WAR ON THE HOME FRONT

EXPERIENCE LIFE IN BRITAIN DURING THE SECOND WORLD WAR

Juliet GARDINER

CARLTON

CONTENTS

INTRODUCTION

THE HOME FRONT WAS A DEFINING EXPERIENCE.

That experience was shared by 48 million people in Britain during the Second World War. Civilians and men and women in the armed forces who were either in training, on leave, waiting to be posted abroad or serving in Britain all endured the hardships and sudden dangers of total war, a "people's war", as it came to be properly called.

It was an experience of regulation and shortages, uncertainty, boredom, fear and anxiety. A time of change – children evacuated, men, and later women, conscripted into the forces or directed into essential war work, of homes disrupted and certainties unsettled, of futures mortgaged – or put on hold. "For the duration" was an official phrase that was soon appropriated to describe any situation in a war that for a long time nobody could see the end of – or predict the outcome of with any certainty – and which would last for nearly six long years.

It could be a tedious, dreary, demoralizing, sometimes frightening, invariably anxious experience for many people in many ways, though for others – particularly the young – it could be a time of opportunity and excitement. For everyone it was also a defining and unforgettable experience. An extraordinary time in which ordinary people submitted to unprecedented control and lack of self-fulfilment, yet discovered a sense of unity that nurtured both the will to win the war and a growing sense of entitlement earned in the years of sacrifice, hard work and selflessness that war demanded. This feeling would be influential in shaping the post-war "people's settlement" when peace finally came, and which is still a shaping force in British life today.

Some aspects of the Home Front were common to all. Everyone endured rationing, the blackout and shortages. Those who were not called to arms nevertheless donned uniforms to serve the country in a myriad of different ways: in Civil Defence, the Women's Voluntary Service, the Boy Scouts and the Royal Observer Corps, among others. For others the war effort consisted of working in munitions factories, digging for victory, having soldiers or evacuees billeted on them,

raising money for the Spitfire Fund or making a contribution by simply carrying on, staying put, making do, staying silent, not panicking and keeping cheerful. These were all things the British government urged on its people, sometimes patronizingly, sometimes with perception and humour, in the full knowledge that civilian morale was as vital to victory as any military strategy. In fact the people's resolve would be the target of the Luftwaffe just as persistently as would military installations, war production factories, airfields or transport and communication links.

The Home Front experience between 1939 and 1945 was one unique in British history: it has been recounted many times, but since it involved the entire nation any narrative weaves a rich, varied, complex – and sometimes contradictory – pattern that can be explored in a variety of ways. The intention of this book is to recount, recall and reproduce that experience as authentically as possible by telling of those wartime experiences that were common to everyone alongside those, such as the occupation of the Channel Islands, working with POWs, registering as a Conscientious Objector or breaking German secret codes, that directly affected only certain people. In writing *War on the Home Front* my aim was to convey the flavour of the Second World War on the home front for all levels of society though a largely chronological account that includes newspaper and magazine reports, letters, photographs, drawings, paintings, propaganda material, maps, plus the ordinary artefacts of daily wartime life, many of which will be evocative to those who lived through the war years and eye-opening to those who came after and who want to understand how it was on the home front now over 70 years ago.

JULIET GARDINER

"BE PREPARED"

"Peace for our time" the Prime Minister, Neville Chamberlain, had promised the British people from the balcony of 10 Downing Street on 30 September 1938, after a frantic visit to Munich in Germany in an attempt to avert the crisis threatening the peace of Europe. Chamberlain and the French premier, Edouard Daladier, had hoped to appease the territorial ambitions of the Nazi leader Adolf Hitler, by agreeing to the German Army taking over the German-speaking frontier areas of Czechoslovakia. In a private meeting later the German Führer and the British Prime Minister had signed a declaration that in future their two countries would consult over any difficulties that might arise between them rather than resort to military action.

Chamberlain believed he had brought back "peace with honour" from Munich. Others were more sceptical, believing that Hitler's actions since 1933, such as tearing up the 1919 Versailles Peace Treaty by withdrawing from the Geneva disarmament conference, building up the German Air Force, remilitarizing the Rhineland and annexing Austria, showed that the Nazi leader could not be trusted, and that his ambitions in Europe would inexorably lead to war. However, the relief felt by the vast majority of British people at the settlement was palpable.

Hitler's occupation of the Rhineland on 7 March 1936, and the Italian Fascist leader Benito Mussolini's invasion of Abyssinia (modern-day Ethiopia) on 4 October 1935, had forced Britain to reconsider its defence policy. In January 1937, the government had allocated £1,500 million for defence over the next five years and

switched its priority to an integrated defence system rather than bomber construction. Nevertheless, by September 1939 the British Army numbered only 897,000 as compared to a total of 4.5 million Germans and only four radar stations were operational. Spitfire fighter planes would also need modification before they would be able to engage Luftwaffe (German Air Force) bombers effectively and there would need to be more of them.

It was expected that war would involve a massive and sustained aerial bombardment of the civilian population. Extrapolating from the First World War air raids on Britain when some 400 tons of

ABOVE *Anderson air raid shelters in sections ready for erection in the back garden, delivered to householders in Muswell Hill, north London.*

BELOW *Advice taken: Londoners carrying their gas masks in the cardboard box provided cross London Bridge on Monday 4 September 1939, the day after war was declared.*

ABOVE *A Ministry of Home Security poster instructing British citizens in the use of their gas masks.*

THE MUNICH SETTLEMENT

Adolf Hitler annexed Austria in March 1938. On 12 September, a violently anti-Czechoslovakian speech by the Führer made it clear where the next German acquisition would be. Russia and France both had treaty obligations to Czechoslovakia, and Chamberlain quickly tried to appease Hitler's demands. After a third meeting with Hitler in Munich on 29 and 30 September, also attended by the French and Italian leaders Daladier and Mussolini, the British, French and Italians agreed to the German Army's occupation of the German-speaking frontier area of Czechoslovakia, an agreement in which the Czech government had no say.

ABOVE *Chamberlain addresses crowds at Heston airport on his return from Munich on 30 September 1938.*

bombs caused 4,820 casualties including 1,413 deaths, predictions of the destruction that the Luftwaffe could inflict on the British people grew each year. By 1937, with evidence not only of Abyssinia but also the bombing by German and Italian forces of Guernica in the Spanish Civil War, the Air Ministry faced the possibility of a massive "knock out blow". This would consist of 3,500 tons of bombs falling in the first 24 hours of the war, and it would be "fair to assume that, in densely populated areas such as London, there will be 50 casualties per ton of bombs dropped. Of these casualties, one-third will be killed and two-thirds wounded". This was the prediction of the Committee of Imperial Defence some years earlier.

Although a secret Air Raid Precautions (ARP) sub-committee had been set up in 1924 to examine "the organisation for war, including Civil Defence, home defence, censorship and war emergency legislation", it was not until January 1938 that the first ARP Act came into force. This compelled local authorities to appoint ARP wardens, set up emergency ambulance services, first aid posts, rescue, repair and demolition services, and expand their local fire services by forming and equipping an Auxiliary Fire Service.

It was not only bombs that preoccupied those concerned with the defence of civilians. Fear of gas attacks, which had been such a terrible feature of the Western Front in 1915–18, was also a consideration. By January 1937, 150,000 gas masks were being assembled every week, and at the time of the Munich crisis in September 1938, 38 million masks had been distributed to civilians, gas contamination stations were set up, and training given on how to detect gas and deal with its deadly effects.

Munich galvanized preparations for war. As well as the distribution of gas masks, trenches were dug in public parks and playing fields, plans were drawn up for evacuation and a population that had hitherto been apathetic towards ARP measures was alerted to the real possibility of war. Thousands volunteered to become ARP wardens, most on a part-time basis, and, in the early days, equipped with a uniform of only a badge, brassard (arm band) and a tin helmet.

In March 1939, German troops occupied the rest of Czechoslovakia: the policy of appeasement lay in tatters and the peace that Chamberlain hoped he had brought back to Britain was fast running out.

BELOW *The news almost no one wanted. A newspaper vendor displays a terse announcement on his billboard on the outbreak of war in September 1939.*

"GET THE CHILDREN AWAY"

The government operation to "get the children away" began on 1 September 1939. It was clear that war with Germany was imminent and the expectation was that bombing raids would begin at once. The key imperative was to get children to safety as quickly as possible.

"Operation Pied Piper", the code-name for the evacuation scheme, was a huge undertaking. The country was divided into "danger zones" such as London, Liverpool, Glasgow and other industrial cities expected to be enemy targets, which were designated for evacuation. Rural and coastal areas considered safe were "reception areas", while the rest of the country was to be neutral, neither sending nor receiving evacuees.

Those agreeing to billet evacuees would receive a modest payment and it was illegal under wartime regulations to refuse if a householder had the room. However, local authorities were naturally reluctant to place a child in a home where he or she was not welcome, and prosecutions were relatively rare.

Although there was no legal obligation on parents to send their children away, pressure was strong to register them for the government scheme. It was a hard decision for those who believed that "surely if war comes it would be better for families to stick together and not go breaking up their homes?".

As well as schoolchildren evacuated with their teachers, mothers (or other carers) of children under five were allowed to take part in the government scheme, as were expectant mothers and the disabled. In addition, thousands had made private arrangements: public schools had taken over stately homes, firms and civil service departments had relocated all over the country, and many families and individuals arranged to stay with friends and relations in the country for the duration.

Given the scale of the enterprise, the evacuation worked surprisingly well. Children set out for mainline train stations carrying a suitcase or pillowcase containing items of clothing which had been prescribed in letters sent out from their schools. They also carried food for the journey and their gas mask in its regulation cardboard box, maybe clutched a favourite toy, and had a label attached to their coat giving their name, number and school. At the stations they were herded on to trains by station staff and willing WVS (Women's Voluntary Service) members to destinations unknown.

BELOW *Children from Myrdle School, Stepney, in London's East End, having assembled in the school playground, are taken to the railway station to be evacuated to the country on 1 September 1939.*

ABOVE *A luggage tag was attached to the lapel of each evacuee giving their name and usually the name of their school but no destination, since that was not known.*

RIGHT *Mothers, who were not allowed on to the railway platform, watch as their children board a train at Waterloo station for "destinations unknown" in the countryside, where it was hoped they would be safe from bombing raids.*

BELOW *A more reassuring approach: a call for volunteers to help with the evacuation of children and provide welcoming billets in the countryside.*

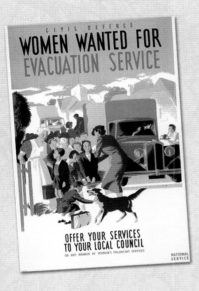

CIVIL DEFENCE

WOMEN WANTED FOR EVACUATION SERVICE

OFFER YOUR SERVICES TO YOUR LOCAL COUNCIL
OR ANY BRANCH OF WOMEN'S VOLUNTARY SERVICES

NATIONAL SERVICE

The problems started when the children reached their destinations. So much attention had been paid to the logistics of getting them away that not enough thought had been devoted to how they would fare when they arrived. In some places it was like a cattle market as billetors wandered round selecting the children they wanted: pretty little girls were soon chosen, while in farming areas, strong-looking lads were most likely to be picked. Many mothers had instructed "you must all stay together", but it was often hard to find a householder prepared to offer a home to two or three or even more siblings.

While some children bonded instantly with their temporary foster parents and look back on their years as an evacuee as a rural idyll, others found the experience traumatic. Some of their billets were entirely unsuitable, some children were neglected, their unhappiness at leaving their families ignored, while a few were treated with actual cruelty. Education could be difficult too, despite the best efforts of teachers, with evacuees cramming into local schools for often half-time schooling, or being taught in village halls with acute shortages of books and material.

It wasn't easy for the host families either, having small, often homesick, strangers landing on them for an indeterminate time. There were complaints – often exaggerated – about the way that some of the "slum" children behaved. When the bombs failed to fall both evacuees' families and their rural hosts began to wonder why they had left the cities and the drift back began, led by mothers with their babies, most of whom found the countryside inhospitable and dull. By December 1939 some 60 per cent of the evacuees had returned home and though there were other forays out of the cities when the Blitz began in September 1940 and again with the V1s and V2s in 1944, there was never another mass government evacuation, and many who had participated in the 1 September exodus declined to repeat the experiment.

> **"** At first it was just like another holiday, **BUT AFTER A TIME a FUNNY FEELING OF HOMESICKNESS seemed to creep into me, and I HOPED AND PRAYED that THE WAR WOULD END. "**
>
> **13-YEAR-OLD ELIZABETH MOSSMAN, AN EVACUEE FROM STREATHAM IN SOUTH LONDON TO SUSSEX**

OVERSEAS EVACUATION

"Wish Me Luck As You Wave Me Goodbye" sang some of the 100 children aboard the SS City of Benares *as it set sail for Canada from Liverpool on 13 September 1940. Most of these "seavacuees" were being sent to safety overseas under the auspices of a new government scheme designed to ensure that it was not only the rich who had this opportunity. But five days out to sea, the* Benares *was torpedoed by a German U-boat: it sank with the loss of 256 lives including 77 children – five from a single family.*

LEFT *Child evacuees board a ship bound for Australia in August 1940 under the short-lived government scheme for overseas evacuation.*

THE PHONEY WAR

Britain at war was a transformed country. On 3 September 1939, a number of wartime regulations were put into effect. The ARP had been mobilized and conscription had been legislated for in April 1939. Soon all over Britain uniformed men – and women who had volunteered for the auxiliary services, the Auxiliary Territorial Service (ATS), the Women's Royal Naval Service (WRNS) or the Women's Auxiliary Air Force (WAAF) – seemed to be everywhere. With thousands of children evacuated to the country, many city streets seemed strangely quiet.

And they were dark. Blackout regulations had been in force since 1 September, so street lamps were extinguished, and cars, buses, trams and trolley buses were obliged to mask their headlights and screen interior lights. At first, it was forbidden to carry a torch, but soon that restriction was relaxed and a torch could be used if covered with two layers of tissue paper and directed at the ground – but soon it was all but impossible to buy a torch battery, such was the demand.

Going out in blackout conditions could be hazardous – road fatalities increased by 100 per cent in the first four months of the war compared to the corresponding months in 1938 and well over half of those were pedestrians. But staying in could be a depressing experience, too. After 3 November 1939, blackout regulations decreed that between half-an-hour after sunset and half-an-hour before sunrise no chink of light should glimmer from any window of any premises – factories, offices, shops or people's homes. There had been a run on blackout material in the last days of peace, and those who could not find any, or could not afford it, resorted to painting their windows black, fashioning makeshift screens or just not switching the lights on.

Those charged with enforcing the blackout were ARP wardens, many of whom came to be regarded as "little 'itlers" as they bawled "Put that light out" to anyone whose obliteration of their lights was less than total. In 1940, 300,000 people across the country were prosecuted for blackout offences.

To add to the gloom, electricity voltage had been reduced, making it more difficult to read, and the BBC had entered into the wartime spirit by shutting down its regional networks (to lessen the airwave traffic) and pulling most

RIGHT *Total war. Sombre news of military, political and civilian activity on the front page of the* Daily Herald *the day after war was declared.*

BELOW *The neon advertisements in London's Piccadilly Circus were switched off in the blackout conditions that pertained for most of the Second World War and did not come back on for some time after the war.*

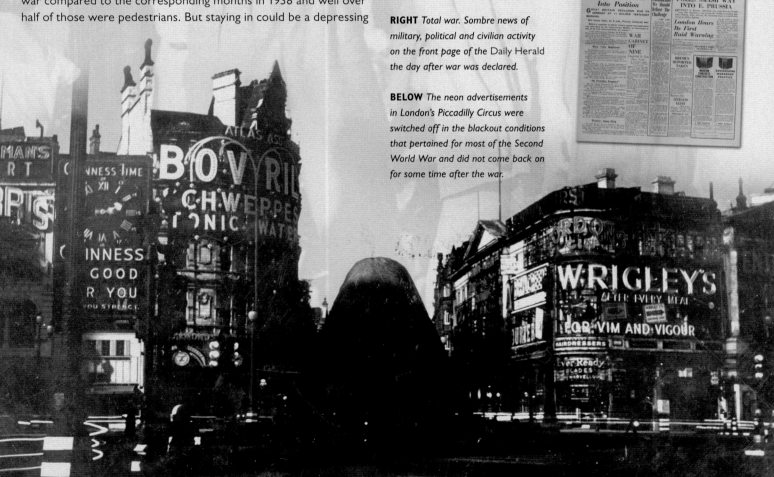

PROTECTING THE HOME

"Is your blackout really black?" asked a popular wartime song. Householders struggled to block out any sliver of light, even though, with planes flying at around 25,000 feet, it was unlikely that a bomber pilot would be able to navigate by a set of undrawn curtains in a suburban street. Other protective precautions included putting a lattice of sticky tape over windows to stop glass flying about after a bomb fell, and many households had a stirrup pump ready in the hall to extinguish incendiary bombs.

ABOVE *A refinement on the usual hastily-run-up blackout coverings was this ventilator device that could be attached to curtains. This allowed air to circulate and relieve the stuffiness of blacked-out rooms such as cinemas or theatres as shown here.*

of its more entertaining programmes. All that could be listened to in the early days of the war were somewhat sententious news bulletins or Sandy Macpherson endlessly playing the organ. Before long, the BBC realized that the wireless was essential to maintaining morale as well as providing information and admonition. It began broadcasting programmes like *ITMA* (*It's That Man Again*), starring Tommy Handley and with a cast of characters including Funf the Spy, and in later series Mrs Mopp, Colonel Chinstrap and Ali Oop, the saucy-seaside-postcard vendor. These gave the nation something to laugh at as well as a whole lexicon of wartime catch phrases.

Those who did venture out in the blackout might wear a flash of white – a silk flower perhaps, or a peeking-out handkerchief – as they walked along pavements with the kerbs painted white. Everyone would be expected, though never legally required, to carry their gas mask in a cardboard container on a piece of string. By the outbreak of war, 44 million "respirators", as they were officially called, had been issued but, despite government posters and leaflets urging people to "Take Care of Your Gas Mask and Your Gas Mask Will Take Care of You", increasingly, people did not carry them. A survey conducted on Westminster Bridge in November 1939 showed that only 24 per cent of men and 39 per cent of women were carrying their gas masks, while in Lancashire on the same day the numbers were six percent of men and nine per cent of women.

Not bothering to carry gas masks was part of a feeling that the "bore war" or, borrowing from America, the "phoney war" as it came to be called, wasn't the war that everyone had been expecting. What was Hitler doing? Where were the bombs that were supposed to decimate Britain as soon as hostilities had been declared? Sandbags outside public buildings were beginning to rot, signs reading "To the shelter" looked redundant, and the Home Front did not seem a battle front at all – yet.

ABOVE *Alert. Two recruits to the ARP at the corrugated-iron shelter that serves as their hut, ready to respond to a call to fire should bombing raids start.*

LEFT *Conscientious staff and customers don gas masks in this posed picture of a gas mask drill in a department store in London's Bayswater in 1941.*

MILITARY SERVICE

In August 1914, the rush to the colours had been such a stampede that, according to *The Times*, mounted police were required to hold the young recruits, eager to fight for King and Country, in check. The scene was very different in September 1939.

For a start there was little enthusiasm for war. Jingoism was notably absent and in its place was a weary acceptance of the inevitability of the coming conflict, a recognition that, for the second time in just over two decades, Britain was at war with Germany. In addition, before the war, government thinking had focused on deterrence and protection. Spending on a defensive air shield and on Bomber Command had taken priority while for years the Regular Army had been starved of resources – and men. Neville Chamberlain had given his word that he would not introduce conscription during peacetime.

Although there had been some recruitment to both the Regular Army and the Territorial Army at the time of Munich, the Prime Minister was finally forced to concede that this was insufficient for the war that threatened – and particularly inadequate to fulfil Britain's treaty obligations to France. In the face of stiff opposition in the country and from 133 Members of Parliament who voted against the measure, the Military Training Act passed into law in April 1939. All men would be liable for call-up in their 20th year: they would be trained and serve full-time for six months, and then be called upon for part-time service in the Territorial Army for a further three and a half years. By September 1939 there were 897,000 men in the army including the Territorial Army.

Paradoxically, this compulsion increased the number of volunteers, since people realized how imminent war was; also, volunteers had the privilege – theoretically, at least – of choosing which service they joined. In fact, although the Royal Air Force (RAF) and the Royal Navy proved the more popular, it was the Army that needed most men, so that is where the majority of the recruits went, regardless of their preference. On the outbreak of

ABOVE *Rodrigo Moynihan, Medical Inspection (1943). Moynihan was a reluctant soldier and in this painting he suggests the routine indignities and numbing regulation of military service.*

RIGHT *War by other means: Conscientious Objectors directed to work on the land attending a Ministry of Agriculture training course in Essex in July 1940.*

war, conscription was extended to men aged between 18 and 41 (raised to 51 in December 1941) and the Territorial Army was, in effect, merged with the Regular Army into a single fighting force. Civilians had to be turned into fighting men indistinguishable from regular soldiers – and "it wasn't done by kindness".

By the end of the war, the British Army had more than tripled in size to nearly three million men; the Royal Navy (including the Royal Marines) stood at 783,000 and the RAF, the newest of the services, had a total strength of 950,000.

Under the terms of the National Service (Armed Forces) Act, which was passed on 1 September 1939 as German troops marched into Poland, all men's names were placed on the Military Service Register, which made them liable for call-up. If a man, for reasons of religious, moral or political conscience, objected to his name being placed on the Register he could apply to be put on the Register of Conscientious Objectors instead. In this case, he would be called before a local tribunal to argue his case. The tribunal had four options. Its members could register the applicant as a Conscientious Objector (CO) with no conditions attached as to what he did; they could register him on condition he undertook work under civilian rather than military control – working on the land was particularly popular – or in the Civil Defence services if he was prepared to; they could remove his name from the CO Register but stipulate that he could only be called up for non-combatant duties in the Armed Forces, maybe serving in the Royal Army Medical Corps or undertaking the hazardous work of defusing unexploded bombs. Finally, they could refuse his request to be placed on the CO Register, in which case the man would be liable for military service.

By the end of 1945 there were 59,192 "conchies", as they were called. This was approximately 1.2 per cent of the five million men "called up" and the majority had objected on religious grounds. Nearly 18,500 men had their applications to be placed on the CO Register rejected: of those 10,878 appealed and eventually 1,891, whose appeals were not successful, went to prison for refusing to undertake military service as directed.

LEFT *"Wish Me Luck as You Wave Me Good Bye". Leave over, couples embrace at Euston station as servicemen prepare to go back to military service.*

BELOW AND BACKGROUND *The everyday cost of conflict. A soldier father kisses his young child goodbye through the bars of a railway-station barrier as he sets off for war.*

RESERVED OCCUPATIONS

Determined not to repeat the mistakes of the First World War, when indiscriminate recruiting of men for the forces left a serious shortage of labour in the war industries, the government had prepared a reserved (or scheduled) occupation scheme in January 1939. It covered some five million men in a wide range of occupations, from boilermakers and lighthouse-keepers to teachers and doctors, with engineering having the most exemptions. Men in reserved occupations were to be exempt from military service, sometimes after a certain age. The scheme had to be revised, with fewer exemptions being allowed, in 1941.

ABOVE *The war effort. A young man testing an amplifier in a factory producing electro-acoustic equipment for the RAF. This would have been a reserved occupation.*

FOOD ON THE RATION

Ration books evoke the Second World War in Britain more than almost anything else. And yet the government was so unsure about the public's reaction to food rationing that it hesitated about introducing it. It was not until Monday, 8 January 1940, after several postponements, that food finally went "on the ration". By that time reports of food hoarding, the experience of shortages and, for some people, memories of the chaotic situation in the First World War caused most housewives to welcome the system.

Every household received a ration book for each member and was required to register with a retailer. Coupons could only be exchanged with that retailer since the shopkeeper received stock replacements based on the number of customers registered with him or, occasionally, her. At first, shopkeepers were expected to snip out the coupons and take them to the local Food Office, but this caused a massive amount of work and was easy to fiddle, so in the end shopkeepers stamped their customers' books instead.

The first items to be rationed were bacon or ham (4oz/115g per person per week), sugar (12oz/340g) and butter (4oz/115g). In March, meat was rationed, with each ration book holder getting 1s 10d (one shilling and ten pence)-worth a week, which in decimal currency is about 9 new pence. The meat ration could be taken as an expensive cut or a larger amount of cheaper meat for braising or stewing. A family could also combine their rations in order to buy a joint or 1s 10d would buy two fair-sized lamb chops in 1940. Cheese was first rationed in May 1941 and preserves (jam and

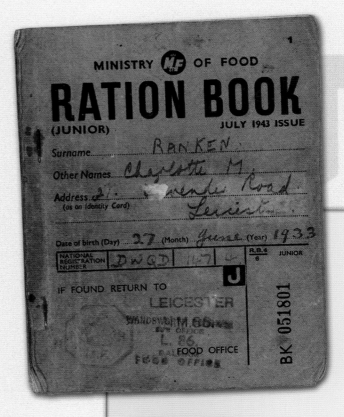

BELOW *A butcher in south London cuts out the necessary coupons from a housewife's ration book on 8 January 1940, the first day of rationing.*

POINTS FOR TREATS

A welcome adjunct to basic food rationing was the "points system" introduced in December 1941. Everyone received the same number of "points" which initially covered tinned fish, meat and beans — non-perishable foods — but soon spread to other items. As points varied according to availability, a housewife could chose to blow them all on a luxury, like a tin of red salmon, or spread them across several "lower points" foods. Sweet and chocolate rationing began on 26 July 1942. At first it was 8oz (226g), it increased to 16oz (453g) and finally settled at 12oz (340g) for a four-week period for the rest of the war.

ABOVE *The ration book for a ten-year-old girl in 1943. A child of that age would be entitled to the same provisions as an adult plus an extra allowance of milk and eggs.*

marmalade), syrup and treacle were rationed to 8oz (225g) a month from March 1941, but from June 1943 the ration could be taken as sugar so that housewives could make their own jams and marmalade. Tea had been rationed since July 1940 and limitations on the "cup that cheers" caused considerable anguish for people; in the same month margarine and cooking fat were rationed, too.

What the coupons could buy varied throughout the war depending on availability: the cheese ration fell to a single ounce (30g) in May 1941, rose again to 8oz (225g) in July 1942 but plummeted down to 3oz (85g) in May 1943. Similarly the meat ration fell to 1s (5p in decimal currency) in March 1941 but went up to 1s 2d in July and remained there for the rest of the war. That seemed particularly irksome to men who regarded meat as a vital body-building food essential for their war work.

The thinking behind rationing was to ensure a fair allocation of food to everyone, and only those foods that could be guaranteed were rationed. Since the supply of eggs and milk was affected by the seasons (hens lay more eggs and cows give more milk in the summer) and could not be guaranteed they were "allocated" rather than rationed and the intention (which it was not always possible to fulfil) was that everyone would get a little less than one egg per week. Dried egg powder in tins was first introduced in June 1942 and one tin (the equivalent of 12 eggs) was allowed every eight weeks. It was useful in cooking but dried-egg omelettes were an acquired taste that many never did acquire.

The milk allowance was progressively cut until March 1942, when it was down to three pints (1.7 litres) a week, but children were permitted more milk, as it was regarded as essential for healthy growth. Children under five were entitled to seven pints of subsidized or free milk a week. After 1942 this ration was supplemented with orange juice and cod liver oil. Children under five had no tea ration and those under six only half the meat allowance. Pregnant women and nursing mothers were entitled to extra milk and vitamin supplements.

There were many items that were not rationed but were not necessarily freely available: offal was one and fish another, and fruit and vegetables were never rationed, although anything exotic like oranges or bananas was virtually unobtainable and if any did come into the shops, they were reserved for children first. Bread was never rationed in wartime – although it was after the war because wheat production was low for several seasons – but the "National Loaf", similar to the modern wholemeal loaf, was deeply unpopular.

Rationing was seen to be an important part of the "People's War" ethos: equality of sacrifice

and fair shares for all, but it was never entirely so. Money as well as coupons was required and there were many poorer families who could never afford to take the full quota of rations to which they were entitled.

ABOVE *Shopkeepers could become quite powerful people as a result of wartime rationing, and it was well worth cultivating a friendship with your local retailer since some scarce foodstuff might be kept "under the counter" for favoured customers.*

LEFT *There were calls for tinned food to go "on the ration" but this was resisted by the Ministry of Food, which introduced a "points" system for such commodities in December 1941 since the supply could not be guaranteed.*

BELOW *The realities of wartime. Leonora K. Green's painting* Coupons Required, 1941, *showing a week's rations for a family after two years at war.*

"DIG FOR VICTORY"

As an island nation Britain might be safer from invasion than her land-locked counterparts, but a naval blockade could force the country to surrender by starving the people of food and resources. In 1939, the British imported more food than they grew, with 90 per cent of cereals and fats and more than 50 per cent of meat coming from abroad. Furthermore, cheap food imports meant that many British farms were entirely given over to pasture, and livestock was otherwise largely fed on imported feed.

Many food imports came to Britain from across the Atlantic. Not only was shipping space on the Atlantic run now required for war matériel and, in the near future, for troops, but the crossing was perilous, with German U-boats (submarines) attacking ships as they ploughed through the ocean. There was no "phoney war" at sea. On the very day that war was declared, 3 September 1939, the *Athenia*, a passenger liner sailing from Glasgow to Montreal, Canada, was torpedoed with considerable loss of life. Six weeks later, on 14 October 1939, a German U-boat managed to sneak into the naval base at Scapa Flow in the Orkneys and sink the battleship *Royal Oak* as it lay at anchor. Magnetic mines threatened British shipping, and in December Nazi planes started to bomb and strafe trawlers as their crews fished in the North Sea. Being as self-sufficient as possible in food was an immediate and urgent wartime imperative. Land had to be turned over to growing corn, potatoes, cattle fodder and other essential foodstuffs.

The Emergency Powers Act of August 1939 empowered the Ministry of Agriculture to control food production, including taking possession of farms or terminating farmers' tenancies if, in the Ministry's view, the land was neglected or inefficiently farmed. So-called "War Agricultural Committees" or "War Ags" were appointed for each county and charged with increasing home food production. A "Plough Now!" campaign was mounted to bring

grassland into cultivation to grow wheat, oats, barley and potatoes to feed the population, and farmers were offered an incentive of £2 an acre to plough up grassland and bring fallow land into cultivation. The aim was to have 1.7 million more acres producing food by harvest-time 1940. The target was reached by April, by dint of farmers ploughing through the night as well as during daylight hours.

The war offered a way out of the low-wage economy endemic among rural workers. Many younger farm workers enlisted in the forces, others were conscripted, and others opted to work in the war industry. The result was that a lack of agricultural labour was a continual wartime problem. However, increasing use of fertilizers and the replacement of horses by tractors and pitchforks by combine harvesters added to the productivity of Britain's rural acres and by 1944 Britain was able to feed itself for roughly 160 days a year rather than the 120 that had been possible at the start of the war.

It was not just large-scale agriculture that was contributing to the nation's self-sufficiency. The herbaceous border, the garden lawn and even the top of the Anderson shelter in the garden were soon enlisted in the "Dig for Victory" campaign. The Cultivation of Land (Allotment) Order of 1939 also empowered local authorities to take over unoccupied land for cultivation and in 1940 an appeal was launched for "half a million more allotments".

TOP *The Ministry of Food humanizes the carrot to encourage people to grow more vegetables to feed their children.*

LEFT *Volunteers in Altrincham, Cheshire pulling up mangolds at night in order to ensure the animal feed crop is gathered in.*

As marginal land was ploughed up for crops, so railway embankments, municipal playing fields, recreation grounds, seaside promenades and any other patch of soil that seemed appropriate (such as the beds surrounding the Victoria Memorial outside Buckingham Palace) was dug and hoed and planted with peas, runner beans, Brussels sprouts, potatoes and anything else that would eke out the family's rations. Some factory owners encouraged their employees to dig allotments on their premises and, after the devastation of the Blitz in 1940–1, enterprising citizens in Britain's cities cleared ground of bomb debris and planted crops in the thin soil among the ruins. Soon rows of carrots competed with the ubiquitous rose-willow herb for space.

By the end of the war there were probably one and a half million allotment holders accounting for 10 per cent of all food produced in Britain, and not only growing vegetables but keeping chickens too, producing at least a quarter of the country's fresh eggs.

BACK TO THE LAND

"Without the food you help to produce the bravery of our fighting services would be of no avail," said the Minister of Agriculture in a radio broadcast urging women *"Back to the Land"*. Nearly 9,000 women had already volunteered for the Women's Land Army by the time war broke out, although at first there had been considerable scepticism among farmers that such *"slips of girls"* could replace the labourers conscripted for war. The work was hard, the hours long and conditions often primitive, but the 80,000-odd *"Land Girls"* were soon seen to be making an invaluable contribution to feeding the nation in wartime.

BELOW *Harvest time: members of the Women's Land Army (known as Land Girls) helping make snooks on a Sussex farm in 1941. The 400-acre field yielded an exemplary thousand tons of wheat.*

ABOVE *The booted foot of Mr McKie of Acton in west London is photographed "Digging for Victory" in a government poster urging the cultivation of gardens and allotments to grow food.*

BELOW *Allotments were dug wherever there was a spare patch of earth such as here in the shadow of the Albert Memorial in Kensington Gardens in 1942.*

A NEW LEADER

By March 1940 the war was six months old. There had been severe losses at sea, conscription was scooping more and more men into the armed forces, there were blacked-out homes and streets, posters and leaflets urging this and warning against that, and ration books had become part of everyone's landscape. And that month the war suddenly seemed much closer. The first civilian was killed in the Orkneys on 16 March, probably by a stray German plane that had mistaken the tiny Scottish hamlet for a nearby airfield. Four days earlier, after battles that had raged since November, Finland had finally signed a peace treaty with the Russian Red Army – and of course the Soviet Union was linked by a non-aggression pact to Nazi Germany.

Despite all this, the Prime Minister, Neville Chamberlain, seemed confident when he told the Central Council of the National Union of Conservative and Unionist Associations on 4 April that things were going well for Britain. The country's fighting capacity was much greater than it had been back in September 1939. Indeed, Chamberlain complacently opined that "Hitler has missed the bus" in failing to take the offensive. They were words that were to haunt him. On 9 April German troops invaded Denmark and Norway. It was, in Winston Churchill's words, "the first crunch of the war".

Norway had declared its neutrality on the outbreak of war. But Germany wanted iron ore from Sweden and other valuable raw materials from Scandinavia. Germany also needed a base for its submarines to fight the Battle of the Atlantic (and later in the war it would need bases for its air and sea operations against Arctic convoys transporting matériel from Britain to the Soviet Union). Already, during the Russo-Finnish War, the French and British had been preparing to send an expeditionary force to the Norwegian port of Narvik. On 8 April, the day when a small British force embarked for Norway, they laid mines around the Norwegian coast to force the German vessels out to fight on the open sea.

WINSTON CHURCHILL (1874–1965)

One of the few British prime ministers to achieve the status of national hero, Winston Leonard Spencer Churchill, a descendant of the 1st Duke of Marlborough, entered Parliament as a Conservative in 1900. Switching to the Liberal Party, he was an energetic Home Secretary and served as First Lord of the Admiralty at the beginning of the First World War. Dogged by charges of maverick behaviour, Churchill, again a Conservative, spent the inter-war years in the political wilderness, when his voice was almost alone in warning against the threat of Nazi Germany. His stand was triumphantly vindicated by his inspiring leadership of Britain at war.

ABOVE *"I knew there was only one person I could send for... who had the confidence of the Country. I sent for Winston and asked him to form a government." King George VI, 10 May 1940*

LEFT *Troops practising boat drill on board the* Oronsay *lying off Gourock at the mouth of the Clyde prior to sailing to join the Norwegian campaign on 20 April 1940.*

ABOVE *A Finnish ski patrol lying in the snow on the edge of a wood in northern Finland, on the alert for Russian troops, on 12 January 1940 during the Russo-Finnish War, fought between November 1939 and March 1940.*

BELOW *The Norwegian Campaign. German destroyers sunk in Narvik harbour by the British battleship* Warspite *and nine destroyers on 13 April 1940.*

The next day, the Germans attacked Norway using combined air, sea and land forces. Airborne troops parachuted in, followed by warships bringing men and supplies, and by lunchtime German forces had seized control of several major Norwegian ports and towns including Narvik and Trondheim. The fight back was a fiasco, under-manned, under-resourced and strategically and tactically flawed. At the beginning of June the Allied troops were evacuated and the King, Haakon VII, and his government fled to exile in Britain.

As First Lord of the Admiralty, Churchill had, to a considerable extent, been the architect of the fiasco. He was also to be its beneficiary. When, on 7 May 1940, it was clear that the Allies were fighting a losing battle, Chamberlain was met with taunts of "missed the bus" as he took his seat in the House of Commons for a debate on the Norwegian Campaign.

It was a bitter occasion. Chamberlain's speech was uninspiring and those of his supporters little better. The First World War hero of Zeebrugge, Admiral Sir Roger Keyes, in service dress, was one critic. Another, the Conservative ex-Cabinet Minister Leo Amery, berated the Prime Minister with the words that Oliver Cromwell had used to the Long Parliament in 1653. "You have sat for too long for any good you have been doing... In the name of God, go!"

When the vote came on the second day of the debate, the Conservative majority had plummeted from 213 to 81. It was clear that Chamberlain no longer commanded the confidence of Parliament, let alone the country. The leader of the Labour Party, Clement Attlee, indicated that his party would be prepared to join a coalition government, but not one led by Chamberlain, the "man of Munich". But there could be no general election in wartime. Who was to succeed him? Lord Halifax, the Foreign Secretary, was the obvious – and King George VI's – choice. But Halifax was tainted by the policy of appeasement and in any case recognized that he did not have the qualities needed to lead the country at such a perilous moment. He advised the King that Churchill was "the better man" for the job. Churchill thought so too. "I felt as if I were walking with destiny," he was to write, as he assumed the offices of both Prime Minister and Minister of Defence on the very day that German tanks smashed into the Netherlands, Belgium and Luxembourg.

DUNKIRK

The British Expeditionary Force (BEF) that was sent to France after the outbreak of war was a small force of some 152,000 men in September 1939 but reached 394,165 by May 1940. Their priority was digging and fortifying a defensive line along the Franco-Belgian border in northern France, where they endured an often cold and wet winter. But their boredom came to a dramatic end on 10 May 1940 as German panzer (tank) divisions invaded Belgium and Holland and then smashed through the supposedly impregnable Ardennes just north of the fortifications of the Maginot defensive line and, further north, over-ran the Netherlands in a matter of days: Holland surrendered on 14 May and Belgium on 28 May.

"We have lost the battle," France's new premier, Paul Reynaud, had told Churchill, as armoured vehicles poured into France. By 20 May, German armoured forces had reached the Channel coast at Noyelles. It was indeed *blitzkrieg* – lightning war – and most of the British and French forces were trapped in a large pocket with their backs to the sea. Seeing no possibility of an effective counter-attack, Lord Gort, Commander-in-Chief of the BEF, took the decision to evacuate his troops. Operation DYNAMO (named after the building dug into the Dover Cliffs which had once housed a dynamo and from where the retreat was co-ordinated) officially started on 26 May although some 28,000 non-essential British personnel had already been evacuated. Long straggling lines of exhausted, battle-shocked, hungry, dispirited and sometimes wounded troops made their way to the beaches by the town of Dunkirk (Dunkerque).

At first chaos reigned: getting the men off the beaches was slow and laborious, discipline frequently broke down as soldiers tried to clamber aboard the boats, and there were reports of officers using their revolvers to keep the men in line. Whenever breaks in the cloud made it possible (which, fortunately, was not very often) Luftwaffe planes shelled and strafed the beaches, inadvertently creating a protective pall of black smoke over the blazing town.

It was a race against time: by May 1940 there were known to be some 400,000 British troops in France. The evacuation was painfully slow until it was decided to get the men on to the boats

"THE LITTLE SHIPS"

From 18 September 1939 radio audiences in Britain and the US could tune into a number of Nazi propaganda broadcasts including those by the notorious William Joyce, nick-named Lord Haw Haw, and many did. To try to counteract the effect of these broadcasts the BBC introduced a series called Postscripts. *A regular contributor was playwright J. B. Priestley, whose broadcast on 5 June 1940 created the legend of the "Dunkirk spirit" and of "the little holiday steamers [that] made an excursion to hell and came back glorious", which rather under-estimated the role played by the Royal Navy and other "big ships".*

ABOVE *"Nothing, I feel, could be more English than the Battle of Dunkirk, both in its beginning and its end, its folly and its grandeur." J. B. Priestley broadcasts to the nation on 5 June 1940.*

BELOW *Survivors of SS* Mona's Queen, *sunk during the evacuation from Dunkirk, await rescue.*

by using the east mole, a sort of breakwater stretching out into the sea, and from which, eventually, two-thirds of the troops got away.

People in Britain were unaware of what was happening, although the pall of smoke could be seen from the south coast, until 29 May, when an appeal went out for vessels to help the hard-pressed Royal Navy get the men away. The response was immediate, although not total – the Rye fishing fleet, for example, ignored the call – and a veritable armada of fishing smacks, pleasure steamers, barges, lifeboats, rowing boats and tugs moved into action under the command of their civilian owners and ex-service personnel. They were the "little ships" that created the potent "spirit of Dunkirk".

It was a hazardous enterprize since the Luftwaffe attacked ships at sea as well as troops on the beach: on 1 June, 31 ships were sunk and 11 damaged as soldiers at sea and troops on the beach asked desperately, "Where's the RAF?". In fact, the RAF had been attacking further inland, its resources were at breaking point, and Air Chief Marshal Sir Hugh Dowding, C-in-C of British Fighter Command, grimly insisted that he must conserve his planes and men for the next battle that he knew would come.

> " Nothing, I feel, could be **MORE ENGLISH THAN DUNKIRK...** the way in which, when apparently **ALL WAS LOST**, so much was **GLORIOUSLY RETRIEVED. "**
>
> J. B. PRIESTLEY, "POSTSCRIPTS", BROADCAST ON 5 JUNE 1940

TOP *Abandoned anti-aircraft guns and shrouded corpses at Dunkirk as British and some French forces are evacuated, leaving behind their heavy fighting equipment and fellow soldiers dead, wounded or taken prisoner.*

LEFT *A straggling line of soldiers wade off the beaches to a waiting destroyer during the evacuation of Dunkirk.*

The evacuation was officially halted on 4 June 1940, leaving some 68,111 men of the BEF killed, wounded or missing in France. The Admiralty estimated that a total of 338,226 men were taken off the beaches, including as many as 118,000 French troops who had believed that the retreat to Dunkirk was to regroup, not evacuate, and who had at first not been allowed on the boats. All the BEF's heavy armour and equipment was abandoned or destroyed.

"Wars are not won by evacuation," Churchill had soberly told the Commons while welcoming the success of the operation. This was, in fact, due in no small part to Hitler's orders on 24 May that the German troops should be conserved to take Paris rather than proceed to the Channel. The BEF's soldiers, too, were concerned at the reception they might receive on their return to Britain after retreating from the first engagement with the enemy. But they need not have worried. Flags and banners and cheering crowds lining the route, many offering cups of tea, sandwiches and cigarettes, proclaimed a hero's welcome.

LEFT *The* Daily Mirror *sets the mood of defiance on 5 June 1940 when it seemed that the battle for France was almost over and the battle for Britain seemed the inevitable next step in Hitler's* blitzkrieg *war.*

THE INVASION SCARE

The mood on the packed benches of the House of Commons on 18 June 1940 was sombre as Winston Churchill pledged that, despite the surrender of the French government the previous day, Britain and its empire would fight on "if necessary for years, if necessary alone". Privately, the recently appointed war leader recognized that Britain's position was perilous – perhaps hopeless. The Army had lost men, morale and equipment in France, and the RAF had lost an estimated 1,393 planes between 10 May and 28 June 1940; bombs were being dropped, admittedly in relatively small numbers, on coastal towns and villages, and shipping in the English Channel and the North Sea was under constant attack. The apparent ease with which the German forces had overrun large areas of western Europe was an ominous portent for Britain's survival. The Channel suddenly seemed a very narrow strip of water and the skies above England appeared invitingly open.

Stories spread like wildfire: German troops would parachute out of the sky dressed as policemen, wearing Allied uniforms, even in nuns' habits; flotillas of barges were, at that moment, assembling along the French coast ready to launch an invasion; the Royal Family had fled to Canada and the British government was packing to leave, too. Patriotic citizens started to wonder what they should do "when the Germans come". In fact, the government was not packing to leave but moving into action.

RIGHT *A badge for "Bundles for Britain". American women knitted garments for British seamen and eventually provided toys, clothing and blankets for civilians in war-torn Britain.*

Signposts were taken down and all place names removed or painted out on roads and at railway stations. Vulnerable stretches of the coast were designated "Defence Areas", children were evacuated from them and anyone who needed to enter one required a permit. Coils of barbed wire festooned the beaches, mines were laid and piers that might have helped the invader to land were partially dismantled. Speculation that could be described as scaremongering was condemned – and could be a reason for arrest. Motorists were instructed to immobilize their car by removing not only the ignition key but also the distributor arm, and anyone who parked a car without removing the ignition key and locking the doors was liable to arrest. Children were forbidden to let off fireworks or fly kites and church bells fell silent, to be rung only to warn of an invasion. Concrete blocks were set up across roads as anti-tank devices and old cars and farm vehicles towed into fields that could have served as landing strips. Newspapers and magazines printed drawings of the German Junkers JU52 since this

> **❝ We shall DEFEND OUR ISLAND, whatever the cost may be, we shall FIGHT ON THE BEACHES, we shall FIGHT ON THE LANDING GROUNDS, we shall FIGHT IN THE FIELDS AND IN THE STREETS, we shall FIGHT IN THE HILLS; we shall NEVER SURRENDER. ❞**
>
> **WINSTON CHURCHILL SPEAKING IN THE HOUSE OF COMMONS, 4 JUNE 1940**

Scanning the horizon for a possible invasion force, men on anti-aircraft lookout duty on board an anti-aircraft ship somewhere off the English coast in August 1940.

was the plane most likely to drop paratroopers, and householders were advised to cut out the drawings and keep them for reference.

A booklet entitled *If the Invader Comes* landed on every doormat in the country on 13 June: it ordered householders to "Stay Put" and be vigilant, refusing to tell or give the invader anything and hiding maps, bicycles and any cans of petrol since "transport… will be the invader's main difficulty". Later, the rather limp instruction to "Stay Put" was amended to the more ringing "Stay Firm", but still instructions as to what people should do (as opposed to should not do) if the Germans landed were vague. It was hard to see how they could be otherwise. Mindful of the way that terrified French families had fled in the path of advancing German troops, clogging the roads and making any counter-attack all but impossible, it seemed imperative to instruct the British not to do that, but it was equally impossible to train

CAMOUFLAGE

It was not only soldiers that needed to be camouflaged in drab uniforms. Given the range of 20th-century reconnaissance techniques and weapons, vital civilian and military installations that could be identified from the air and then attacked needed to be disguised, too. During the Second World War scientists, including the zoologist Hugh Cott, dress designer Victor Stiebel, the surrealist painters Julian Trevelyan and Roland Penrose, the magician Jasper Maskelyne and others, were recruited to develop sophisticated techniques of concealment and deception, such as disguising pill boxes as tea rooms, petrol stations or public lavatories.

ABOVE *Coastal gun batteries at Kessingland, Suffolk, camouflaged so that they look like holiday-camp chalets, August 1941.*

and arm an entire population to resist and, in any case, no one knew where the assault might come or on what scale.

In fact, Hitler had been advised that far from being a natural follow-up to the conquest of France, the invasion of Britain was a last resort, only to be contemplated when the country had been brought to its knees by a naval blockade and attrition from the air. His Commander in Chief of the Navy, Admiral Erich Raeder, did not consider that an invasion of Britain was feasible, given the large number of special landing craft that the Germans would have needed and did not have, and the extreme difficulty of landing men across a wide front and pressing them inland through heavily defended country.

Although the Führer still entertained the illusion that once Britain realized the hopelessness of its position, its leaders would sue for peace, he issued orders, called Operation SEALION, to prepare for the invasion of Britain on 16 July 1940. The order was indefinitely postponed on 17 September 1940, by which time Hitler's focus had turned eastwards to Russia. Operation SEALION was not formally abandoned until February 1942.

ABOVE LEFT *To confuse the enemy, signposts that might be of use to an invading army are removed by Civil Defence workers on 31 May 1940.*

BELOW *Baths and water troughs being dragged onto the fairways of a golf course (location unknown) to prevent enemy aircraft from landing during the invasion scare of 1940.*

THE HOME GUARD

Immediately after the nine o'clock news on 14 May 1940 Anthony Eden, the Secretary of State for War, offered the opportunity to "countless ordinary citizens especially those not eligible to enrol in the armed forces, who had asked to be allowed to serve in the defence of their country in its hour of peril" to join in the formation of a body that would come to be immortalized as "Dad's Army". He called the new organization Local Defence Volunteers (LDV). Volunteers would not be paid, said Eden, "but you will receive uniforms [which they did, eventually] and you will be armed" [which they were, in the even more distant future]. Men were instructed to register at their local police station. Within 24 hours of the broadcast some quarter of a million had done so and by the end of June the number of volunteers stood at one and a half million, far more than Eden, or anyone else, had expected.

The range of volunteers was impressive, from the local MP to farm labourers, and all were prepared for action – and for hours of drill and exercises in the evenings and at the weekends to turn this motley crew of volunteers into a force to defend the homeland. The bulk of volunteers were men too old for military service and included a high percentage of ex-servicemen, some of very high rank indeed, while others were under age for soldiering, or in a reserved occupation, engaged in work that was regarded as essential to the war effort and therefore not liable for military service. At first, membership was voluntary, but from November 1941 all men aged between 18 and 54 who were not in the armed forces or other Civil Defence work were compelled to serve part-time in the Home Guard.

RIGHT *A home-made hand grenade made by a member of the Home Guard eager to repel enemy invaders.*

Since there were not sufficient weapons for the Regular Army after Dunkirk, supplying it had to take priority, and most LDVs were forced to train with whatever came to hand, including broom handles, garden hoes or maybe a First World War Lee Enfield rifle if they were lucky. And the "uniform" consisted for some time of nothing more than a brassard stencilled with the letters LDV. Even these had to be changed when Churchill, who argued that Local Defence Volunteers was hardly a name to inspire, got his way and on 20 July 1940 it was declared that the force would be known as the Home Guard.

The lack of weapons continued to be a pressing issue. Volunteers were instructed on how to make "Molotov cocktails" by filling bottles with petrol, paraffin, benzine or creosote to

BELOW *The Springfield (Essex) Home Guard take part in a bayonet charge during training in a local park.*

lob at approaching German tanks, and in desperation the War Office started to issue truncheons in June 1941. A quarter of a million primitive "bayonets", consisting of a long metal tube with a blade welded on the end, were distributed the following month – to almost universal derision. Other Heath Robinson-like contraptions that were developed included the so-called "Woolworth Bomb" – essentially a lump of gelignite in a biscuit tin, the Northover Projector (named after its inventor) that only cost £10 to manufacture and fired grenades using toy pistol caps, and the Blacker Bombard (later renamed the less medieval-sounding Spigot Mortar) which could – sometimes – deliver a 20lb anti-tank mortar bomb.

RIGHT *Members of the Home Guard stand at ease during a parade outside All Saints Church, Springfield. Their rifles are fixed with bayonets.*

BELOW *Members of the Home Guard take advantage of the protection offered by some medieval battlements during a training exercise with regular army units in the Boroughbridge area of Yorkshire in June 1941.*

Fortunately, such primitive weaponry never had to be deployed to defend the United Kingdom, but it did raise the question: what was the Home Guard for? The nagging feeling persisted that the government had made a grand gesture to boost morale without much thought as to how the men were to be deployed and equipped. Were they to "harass and attack the enemy" in the event of an invasion on home soil with the intent of "maiming or killing him"? Or was their role be more like that of a special constable, to observe, check and report?

If German troops had invaded and occupied Britain, the Home Guard would most likely have been regarded as *franc-tireurs*, an armed militia, and its members shot. Had the invasion happened, this ill-equipped, often over-zealous force, a mixture of old soldiers and those who had never encountered military discipline before, would have been called upon to defend their country. Their responsibilities would have been awesome and the dangers they faced formidable, since the Home Guard was instructed to "hold their allotted positions to the last man and the last round to enable the Field Army to destroy the enemy…".

WOMEN AND THE HOME GUARD

The Prime Minister, Winston Churchill, frequently pointed to the "home" part of the Home Guard name as signifying both country and the place where a person lived. Despite this, that portion of the population most associated with "home" – women – were consistently denied membership, although they were often called on to type letters, deliver leaflets or provide tea and buns. Three doughty women MPs fought their corner, but not until April 1943 did the manpower shortage lead to a grudging concession that women aged between 16 and 65 could be nominated by recognized bodies, such as the WVS, as Home Guard auxiliaries.

RIGHT *In February 1942, the magazine* Picture Post *ran a story "Women Sign on for Home Defence" about women who decided to take matters into their own hands to train in defence of their country.*

THE CHANNEL ISLANDS

In the spring of 1940, the Jersey Tourist Board promoted Jersey as the ideal holiday destination for Britons seeking sun and sand. "Happily our Island is far removed from the theatre of war," rejoiced the brochure. But not for long. On 28 June 1940, the Germans bombed Jersey and Guernsey, killing 38 people. Between 30 June and 3 July German forces occupied the four islands of the Channel Islands: the only British soil to be under Nazi occupation and a template perhaps of what would have happened if Operation SEALION had been put into effect successfully and Hitler's troops had marched through mainland Britain's towns and cities.

Since the British government regarded the small cluster of Channel Islands (with Alderney lying only seven miles from the Cotentin peninsula in France) as being of no strategic importance, it had concluded that, with the French coast in enemy hands, all troops, anti-aircraft guns and fighter aircraft would be needed to defend the mainland. If the Germans landed, the Channel Islands should surrender. British forces would not be sent to defend them, even though Churchill regarded it as "repugnant now to abandon British territory which [has] been in the possession of the Crown since the Norman Conquest".

Some 23,600 islanders were evacuated out of a population of 90,000. By December 1941, there were 21,000 Germans stationed in the Channel Islands and by mid-1942 the total was alleged to have

RIGHT A "V for Victory" slogan, inspired by the BBC campaign for subversive acts in occupied Europe, in a St Helier street. Any islander caught defacing a sign in this way would be liable to arrest and imprisonment.

reached 36,960, though it is doubtful that so many were posted there. For five years almost all islanders had daily contact with the occupying forces and many had soldiers billeted in their homes.

It was supposed to be a "model occupation" since, for Hitler, the Channel Islands were a laboratory for the occupation of Britain. The islanders had pragmatic reasons for wanting to be able to continue with their lives as normally as possible, despite having been effectively abandoned by the British government, which had little advice to give. The only recommendation from the British government was that local officials should "administer the government of the Islands to the best of their ability in the interest of the inhabitants". In practice, since the Germans had force on their side, they could requisition what they wanted. A "model occupation" came to mean that the island authorities largely implemented occupation policies, including the regulation of food production and providing labour for German projects, some of them of a military nature.

By 1944, probably three-quarters of the Channel Islands' population were working directly or indirectly for the Germans. Pounds, shillings and pence were replaced by Reichsmarks and pfennigs, villages were given German names, all associations had to be registered with the *Feldkommandantur* and permission was required for meetings. Furthermore, all publications had to be scrutinized by the censor and German propaganda was inserted in the press. Libraries removed any books that might be said to constitute "hate propaganda", such as those by

> **" To think we SACRIFICED more than TEN THOUSAND MEN for one line of trenches and yet DID NOT FIRE A SHOT to save these islands."**
>
> **LORD MOTTISTONE SPEAKING IN THE HOUSE OF LORDS ON 9 JULY 1940, QUOTING AN OFFICER WHO SERVED IN THE FIRST WORLD WAR**

LEFT Sieg im Westen (Victory in the West), a Nazi propaganda film showing at the Gaumont Palace cinema in Guernsey.

Winston Churchill or H. G. Wells, and in March 1942 it was made compulsory for all children over ten to learn the German language.

Between September 1942 and February 1943 a total of 2,200 Islanders were deported to German internment camps. This figure included 200 as a reprisal for a British commando raid and those deported were mainly born outside the Channel Islands. Island officials supplied the names of all Jews living on the islands, their identity cards were stamped with a red "J", Jewish businesses were closed down and most of the Jews "disappeared", to be traced years later to the concentration camps and extermination.

For the ordinary islanders life grew increasingly harsh. Food was scarce – potatoes and bread were rationed as they never were in Britain – and weeks could pass without there being any meat to eat. Medicines were all but unavailable, fuel was almost non-existent, communal ovens were set up and by Christmas 1944 there was no electricity on the islands. Reprisals were taken against any acts of resistance and punitive fines and prison sentences were imposed for relatively minor misdemeanours.

But it was not just the terrible material conditions that marked wartime life in the Channel Islands. There were also the bitter divisions in a once tight-knit community. Accusations of profiteering, black-market activities and collaboration with the enemy were rife, and many in high places were accused of feathering their own nests. Fear, powerlessness, the need to compromise to survive, all the painful moral complexities of an occupied country, were rampant in the occupied Channel Islands, which were not liberated until 9 May 1945, the day after Victory in Europe.

"CORRECT RELATIONS"

The Bailiffs of the Channel Islands instructed citizens to maintain "correct relations" with the occupying German troops. But the spectrum between polite detachment and fraternization was wide and allowed many very different interpretations of "correct relations". Many people came to see the German soldiers simply as "ordinary men" caught up in war. Some local women discovered that the men could have charming manners and a fine physique, and be very generous with food and entertainment. Many had affairs, the illegitimacy rate rose dramatically, and animosity towards these so-called "Jerrybags", or "horizontal collaborators", was yet another divisive effect of occupation.

ABOVE A number of Channel Island women found the smart uniforms, good manners and generous gifts of the occupying German soldiers hard to resist.

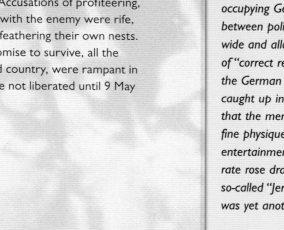

BELOW A Reich War flag flies atop a building on Jersey during the occupation of the Channel Islands.

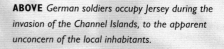

ABOVE German soldiers occupy Jersey during the invasion of the Channel Islands, to the apparent unconcern of the local inhabitants.

27

SPITFIRE SUMMER

"I expect that the Battle of Britain is about to begin," Winston Churchill told the House of Commons after the fall of France. "The whole fury and might of the enemy must very soon be turned on us. Hitler knows that he will have to break us in this island, or lose the war." Churchill was anticipating the attempt of the German High Command to gain air superiority over southern England and to weaken the morale of the British people, which were both essential prerequisites, as the Führer saw it, for the invasion of Britain.

The battle was never clear-cut but is usually judged to have begun in mid-July 1940. From then on, dog fights between the RAF and Luftwaffe wheeled and screamed in the skies above the Home Counties until September, although there had been sorties before June and daylight raids would engage British fighter planes well into the autumn.

European operations had severely depleted Fighter Command's strength: it had only 520 planes fit for operations on 19 June 1940. One of Churchill's first actions on becoming Prime Minister had been to appoint the Canadian-born newspaper magnate Lord Beaverbrook to sort out the "muddle and scandal of aircraft production". "The Beaver"'s motto was "Work without Stopping" and that is what he drove his workforce to do in the dark days after Dunkirk. It was an unsustainable regime since the productivity of exhausted men and women was bound to drop, but between January and April 1940, 2,729 aircraft

ABOVE *Members of the Women's Auxiliary Air Force (WAAF) plot the movement of aircraft in the Operations Room at 10 Group, Box Colerne, Wiltshire, watched by superior officers.*

ABOVE LEFT *Badge of the Fleet Air Arm, the air wing of the Navy, which sent men and machines to the Battle of Britain.*

BELOW *The iconic picture of the "Few". Battle of Britain pilots scramble to their planes in the summer of 1940.*

> **" ' NEVER in THE FIELD of HUMAN CONFLICT was SO MUCH owed by SO MANY to SO FEW.' The words BURNED into MY BRAIN... "**

WINSTON CHURCHILL TO MAJOR-GENERAL "PUG" ISMAY AFTER A VISIT TO OPERATIONS ROOM, 11 GROUP FIGHTER COMMAND ON 16 AUGUST 1940

were produced (638 of which were fighter planes) and from May to August 1940, 4,576 aircraft were made (1,875 of them fighter planes). These could certainly not all be credited to Beaverbrook: production had been under way before he arrived on the scene, but at the same time the Germans were producing around half that number. In addition, the Minstry of Aircraft Production managed to get 1,872 damaged fighter planes back into service between May and August 1940.

However, the shortage of planes was not the RAF's only or, indeed, main problem: lack of people was. Ground staff were in short supply, as were people working on the communications side of operations. And there was a shortage of pilots – Churchill's "Few" – to fly the planes. Training had been speeded up when an over-estimate indicated that the Luftwaffe had at least 7,300 pilots in operational units; from June 1940, 115 new pilots passed out every two weeks. This force was supplemented by airmen from overseas who had fled the German advance in Poland, France and the Netherlands or, like Americans, Canadians and others from the Commonwealth, had volunteered or been posted to Britain. Despite all this, Fighter Command's projection was that by September 1940 it would have 60 squadrons ready for action, when the Air Ministry calculated that 120 squadrons were needed.

It took only six minutes for German bombers to cross the Channel and only another ten before they were over 11 Group's sector airfields (where the main attack was likely to fall) with its HQ at Stanmore in Middlesex. Against this, it took four minutes for radar information of a massed attack to reach the squadrons – even then it was hard to discern the size and height of an approaching bomber formation – and it took a further 13 minutes for a Spitfire to get to a sufficient height to engage German planes. Fortunately, for the first couple of months of the battle, the Luftwaffe concentrated its attacks on shipping in the Channel and light raids on south coast ports; by the time Hitler ordered the Luftwaffe to concentrate attacks on UK airfields, experience of German tactics enabled the RAF to mount more effective multi-squadron attacks on enemy planes.

Bad weather on "Adlertag" ("Eagle Day", 13 August), the start of the operation to "wipe the British Air Force from the skies", meant that the major German attack was largely ineffective. In subsequent weeks repeated heavy raids on airfields such as Biggin Hill,

SALVAGE!

"Waste paper isn't rubbish. It's precious… Remember that one newspaper makes three 25-pounder shell cups… one soap powder canister four aero engine gaskets…" urged the Ministry of Supply. Indeed, very little could be classified as "rubbish" in wartime. Just as saucepans, kettles and fish slices were called upon to manufacture Spitfires, so rags, bones, jam jars, string and scraps of wool could all be used for something, while vegetable waste would feed the neighbourhood pig. By 1944 it was estimated that each household in the country had produced around half a ton of salvage and the "cog scheme" enrolled children to help collect it.

ABOVE *Kettles, saucepans and other domestic aluminium equipment collected for Beaverbrook's "Saucepans into Spitfires" initiative are smelted in a foundry "somewhere in Britain".*

Hornchurch, West Malling and North Weald brought Fighter Command perilously close to defeat. However, Hermann Göring, the German Air Minister and Commander in Chief of the German Air Force, overestimated the success of his operations, believing that Fighter Command was even more thinly stretched than it was.

Between 10 July and 31 October the RAF lost about 915 aircraft, and the Luftwaffe 1,733. On what is known as "Battle of Britain Day", 15 September 1940, the RAF shot down or destroyed 60 planes (although it claimed 185) and damaged 19. But by then, in response to a British bombing raid on Berlin on 25 August, the German leadership made the strategic error of switching the attack from bombing airfields to blitzing London and other cities.

ABOVE *"Beware!" A souvenir from a German plane that crashed in southern England in the summer of 1940.*

LEFT *To many civilians living in the south of England, the Battle of Britain was characterized by these patterns of criss-crossing vapour trails made by British and German aircraft.*

THE ENEMY WITHIN

Since Hitler's coming to power in Germany in 1933 there had been a growing stream of refugees to Britain, the majority of them Jewish, fleeing from Nazi persecution in Germany and Austria. Although the government insisted that Britain was primarily a country of transit and that most of these refugees were only accepted on a temporary basis, some 50,000 adult refugees had registered in Britain between January 1938 and July 1939, along with 7,752 children. This is probably an underestimate of those in the UK, as some refugees did not arrive through official channels and did not register.

On the outbreak of war those aliens whose presence in wartime might be considered to constitute a risk to British security were rounded up and interned. There were around 300 of them, with rabid Nazi fanatics being detained alongside those who had fled Hitler's anti-Semitic atrocities, hoping to find a safe haven in Britain.

In addition, all 73,355 Germans and Austrians over the age of 16 in the UK were obliged to appear before special tribunals. Those categorized by the tribunal as class "A" (of which there were 569) were interned as a possible security risk; those in category "B" (6,782) were subject to various restrictions and kept under supervision, while those in category "C" (66,000, of whom 55,457 were recognized as being refugees from Nazi oppression) had no restrictions placed on them.

BELOW *Corralled behind barbed wire and under the surveillance of an armed guard, so-called "enemy aliens" interned in an unfinished housing estate at Huyton in Liverpool in May 1940.*

RIGHT *A group of the 3,500 German and Austrian women – some with young children – on their way to internment on the Isle of Man on 29 May 1940.*

After 10 May 1940, the day of the German invasion of Belgium and the Netherlands, rumours began to spread that "fifth columnists" had helped the invaders (as they had in Norway) and Churchill argued for a mass internment of aliens. "It would be much better that all these people should be put behind barbed wire," he said. The Home Secretary, Sir John Anderson, at first resisted but by 27 May all category "B" males aged between 16 and 70 were being rounded up, as were all category "B" German and Austrian women aged 16 to 60, unless they were infirm, pregnant or had dangerously ill children.

On 10 June, Italy declared war on Britain and France. The next day, Churchill ordered that all male Italians between 17 and 70 who had been resident in Britain for less than 20 years were to be interned. "Collar the lot" was his phrase.

Internees were confined in camps on racecourses and on an unfinished housing estate at Huyton near Liverpool, but most were sent to the Isle of Man to pass the pointless days in requisitioned hotels and boarding houses. Some were shipped overseas to Canada or Australia in appalling conditions. On 2 July, the *Arandora Star*, crammed with German, Austrian and Italian internees, was hit by a German torpedo and sunk with the loss of over 600 internees, among them some notable anti-fascists.

By mid-July 1940, some 30,000 men and women had been interned but pressure was mounting in Parliament, among some church leaders and in a few newspapers, and without a formal announcement the internment of enemy aliens almost entirely ceased. In August, internees began to be released; by February 1941 more than 10,000 had been freed and the following summer only 5,000 remained in the camps. Many of those released subsequently served in the British armed forces or volunteered for Civil Defence or other war work.

In that fearful summer of 1940, potential "enemies within" were identified among Britain's native population, too. Defence Regulation 18B, passed on 1 September 1939, allowed the authorities to detain those whom they believed were capable of prejudicial acts against the State without specifying charge, trial or length of sentence.

While refugees from Hitler's Germany might be interned, the 22,500 or so members of Sir Oswald Mosley's British Union (BU) were considered to be merely a nuisance rather than a threat

OSWALD MOSLEY (1896–1980)

As Labour Chancellor of the Duchy of Lancaster, Oswald Mosley "devised an economic solution… to the intractable problem [of unemployment]" in 1930. It was rejected. Mosley resigned and formed the "New Party". The party enjoyed no success in the 1931 General Election, so Mosley turned to extra-parliamentary methods, founding the British Union of Fascists in 1932. In 1936 he added the more supposedly patriotic "and National Socialists" but henceforth his organization was known as the British Union. A charismatic, intellectually arrogant orator, Mosley surrounded himself with blackshirt thugs and his meetings became increasingly violent and anti-Semitic, alienating more moderate supporters.

ABOVE *Sir Oswald Mosley takes the salute at a line-up of black-shirted members of the British Union prior to the notorious "Battle of Cable Street" when the Fascists were involved in violent clashes with Jews, Communists and East Enders on 4 October 1936.*

and the BU's activities were not proscribed nor were its leaders interned until May 1940. On 22 May, Regulation 18B was amended to cover any member of a fascist or proto-fascist organization. The following day, Mosley was arrested and taken to Brixton prison, though he denied that there was any "shred of evidence that I would play the traitor to my country".

In total, 747 BU members were imprisoned, 96 of them women, including Mosley's wife, Diana, who was a dedicated fascist and occasional guest of Hitler. The Mosleys remained in prison until November 1943, never knowing when they might be freed, while Captain Archibald H. Maule Ramsay, Conservative MP for Peebles, was not able to resume his seat in the Commons until his release in September 1944.

LEFT *A rally of the British Union of Fascists and National Socialists held at Earl's Court Exhibition Hall, then the biggest indoor hall in England, on 16 July 1939, at which Mosley appealed to the government in a speech lasting for two hours to "put Britain first", maintaining that "a million Britons shall never die in your Jews' quarrel".*

THE LONDON BLITZ

The war that Britain had been waiting for finally, ominously, arrived on 7 September 1940. There had been air raids before: indeed, by the first anniversary of the outbreak of the war almost 4,000 civilians had been killed or seriously wounded as a result of enemy action. But "Black Saturday" was of a different order altogether. It was the start of the Blitz. For Londoners there would be no respite from air raids for 57 consecutive nights, and the bombers often came over during daylight hours, too.

Frustrated at the resilience of Britain's fighter forces during the Battle of Britain, Hitler had decided to switch the main force of the Luftwaffe assault. London would be the initial target, but within weeks the bombers would also fan out to launch relentless attacks on ports, industrial installations and transport and on communication links around most of Britain's major cities.

It was soon after 16:00 on 7 September when the azure-blue skies of Kent and Surrey suddenly darkened with what seemed like thousands of planes all making straight for London. The sirens wailed in the capital at 16:43 and within minutes bombs had started to rain down on London's docklands in the East End. A huge pall of smoke could be seen from miles away as every fire engine in the metropolis made its way to the East End, where

warehouses were ablaze, their molten contents spilling out on to the roads, making it difficult for the fire fighters to get through to train their hoses on the inferno.

At 18:00 the All Clear sounded and dazed East Enders emerged into a world transformed, with fires burning out of control and masonry crashing to the ground. But the respite was brief: the conflagration acted as a marker and just after 20:00 some 250 German bombers droned overhead. When the All Clear finally sounded again at 04:30 there were 1,000 fire engines in the Royal Victoria Dock area alone: it seemed as if the "whole bloody

THE NIGHT OF 29 DECEMBER 1940
The Luftwaffe came back in force after Christmas 1940. London suffered worst that night. Since it was a Sunday, businesses were deserted and soon "the whole of London seemed alight" with nearly 1,500 fires burning, many out of control.

KEY

High-explosive bombs

Areas of intense incendiary bombing

Regent's Park

BELOW *On 15 October 1940 a bomb fell in Balham High Street, causing the underground station to collapse and forming a 60-foot-wide crater across the High Road, into which this bus fell. 68 people were killed in the station.*

LEFT *St Paul's Cathedral on the night of 29 December 1940 when a heavy raid on the City of London threatened the famous Wren church. It survived and became a symbol of Britain's resolve to "take it" during the Blitz.*

ABOVE *"We can take it." King George VI and Queen Elizabeth visiting an area which had been heavily bombed and talking to the survivors and other local people in April 1941.*

world was on fire", according to one fireman. There was no gas, electricity or water, fires continued to burn and buildings to crash to the ground. Amazingly, the death toll was 430 dead and 1,600 seriously injured: it seemed almost impossible that so many could have survived the horror.

That first night set the pattern for the Blitz: first the Germans would drop incendiary bombs to start fires which would guide the second wave of bombers with their cargoes of high-explosive bombs. In the first week, the East End, with its complex of docks and light industry set hugger mugger with cheaply built dwellings, suffered worst. There was concern in high places that "if the Germans had the sense not to bomb west of London Bridge there might be a revolution in this country". But by mid-September the West End was getting it too. On 9 and 13 September, Buckingham Palace was hit. On 17 September, 350 tons of bombs were dropped on London, more than the total tonnage that had fallen during the First World War. John Lewis's department store on Oxford Street was burnt out, as were many other small shops and businesses throughout the capital.

After Christmas there was a heavy raid on the City on 29 December which threatened St Paul's Cathedral, by then the symbol of British defiance, and left many historic buildings flattened. Cold weather gave Londoners a short respite, but in March almost nightly raids started with increased ferocity and in mid-April came the heaviest raids so far when more than 60 buildings, including the Houses of Parliament, the Law Courts and the Admiralty, were hit, as were 66 of London's boroughs. A total of almost 2,400 Londoners were killed in two raids on 16 and 19 April 1941, including many ARP workers who died in the line of duty.

Even this carnage and destruction was exceeded by the raid of 10 May 1941, almost eight months to the day after the Blitz had started. This time the debating chamber of the House of Commons was destroyed, the Mansion House was badly damaged, 14 hospitals were hit, 2,000 fires burnt that night from the East End to Westminster and nearly 1,500 people lost their lives in a single night. Although no one knew it at the time, this was to be the final major assault of the Blitz on London.

LEFT *Badge of the National Fire Service. The regular fire brigades were merged with the wartime Auxiliary Fire Service in August 1941.*

THE BLITZ IN THE PROVINCES

London was not alone in its agony: few cities and large towns escaped the Luftwaffe's attention even if the raids were not major ones. By 31 December 1940 London had been attacked 126 times and Liverpool 60. In the Midlands, the hub of Britain's war production, Birmingham had experienced 36 raids and Coventry 31. Each experienced a devastatingly heavy attack in November, with 568 dead in Coventry on the night of 14–15 November and almost 800 killed in an 11-hour raid on Birmingham on 22–23 November that started 600 fires.

Ports were another obvious target. Merseyside, with its granaries, power stations and dry docks, was "Hitler's number-one target" outside London, enduring 60 separate attacks up to the end of 1940. On 28–29 November, more than 350 tons of high-explosive bombs, 30 land mines and 30,000 incendiary bombs rained down. The raiders came back on 20 December and returned again the next night, a pattern of attack that was becoming standard. Over the two nights 700 people were killed, 74 when a public shelter in Anfield received a direct hit.

Bristol, another port, had been considered "safe", too far west for the Luftwaffe to bother with, and the city was housing thousands of evacuees as well as many departments of the BBC, which had relocated there. But on the night of 24–25 November, a six-hour raid laid waste to the central shopping area and, due to a shortage of fire equipment and men, several historic buildings were burnt.

All around the country it was the same: three raids on Aberdeen, four on Edinburgh, 11 each on Cardiff and Swansea. The naval towns of Plymouth and Portsmouth (13 times each) were predictable targets, as were Southampton and Hull. Even Hastings was bombed four times in 1940.

The steel-making city of Sheffield was the target for Operation CRUCIBLE in December. Commercial life was severely disrupted and 6,000 people made homeless. Manchester, one of Britain's largest cities and a vital industrial centre, was left looking "like the ruins of Ypres" after a two-night raid on 22–24 December.

As the year turned, it grew bitterly cold: firemen's hoses froze, icicles hung from buildings and engines were immobilized by below-freezing temperatures. The raids continued, with ports and coastal towns once more the Luftwaffe's prime targets. Destruction and death revisited places that had already been decimated, and a new list of locations was added to the mournful litany of devastation and loss. The bombers came back to Liverpool in March, the docks being the main target. Almost 200 people were killed in Wallasey, but Birkenhead suffered the most with three hospitals hit and 264

ABOVE *Manchester aflame. On 22–23 December 1940 Manchester joined the unwelcome ranks of blitzed British cities. Four hundred fires burned, many out of control.*

BELOW *Merseyside was second only to London in the devastation caused by the German Luftwaffe in 1940–41. This photograph, taken a year later, shows the centre of Liverpool razed by bombs and gutted by fires.*

killed. And the toll mounted: for the first eight nights in May the city was bombed unremittingly. On the night of 3–4 May almost 300 bombers converged on Liverpool, sinking ships and blocking the harbour; all over Merseyside fires burned out of control. A total of 2,500 troops were drafted in to help clear up. In that terrible "May Week" 1,900 Merseysiders were killed, 1,450 seriously wounded and some 70,000 people made homeless.

Glasgow, Britain's second-largest city with its heavy industry and shipbuilding, had hoped that Clydeside was out of range of the bombers, but it was attacked in March and again in April and May. The city was so heavily bombed that only eight out of Clydeside's 12,000 houses escaped damage and over 1,000 people were killed. Belfast, which had held similar hopes, had them shattered by devastating attacks in April 1941 that left more than 1,000 dead and factories, shipyards and housing in ruins.

Plymouth had suffered intermittent raids since July 1940, but in March and April 1941 the "civic and domestic devastation exceeds anything we have seen," reported a Mass-Observation team. In total 932 people had been killed and it seemed that "scarcely a house was habitable".

What was to prove the final phase of the Blitz, before Hitler redeployed his forces to invade the USSR, targeted Birmingham again, and Nottingham was bombed on 8 May 1941, perhaps mistaken for Derby where the Rolls-Royce factory was sited. By this time Britain's counter-measures, including anti-aircraft guns and the newly operational Beaufighter plane, were more effective but German losses were still low: probably only around 600 Luftwaffe bombers were lost during the Blitz and many of those crashed in bad weather rather than being shot down. Nevertheless, despite the high toll of British deaths, injuries and destruction, Hitler's attempt to damage the British war economy fatally and break the will of its people had failed.

IRELAND AND THE WAR

While the Irish Free State (Eire) maintained a position of neutrality during the Second World War, some bombs were accidentally dropped on Dublin, and Northern Ireland, part of the United Kingdom, was caught up in the war. On 15–16 April 1941 Belfast was the target of a major raid. Around 950 were killed and 600 seriously injured. On 4 May, the bombers returned to target the docks and shipyards again, killing and injuring civilians. As a result of the two raids, 56,600 houses were damaged, 3,200 being totally demolished, in a city that already had an acute housing problem.

ABOVE *Royal Welsh Fusiliers help clear debris from the streets of Belfast, Northern Ireland after the devastating air raids of April 1941. Fire crews had driven from the Republic that night to help fight fires in the North.*

LEFT *"Nothing I had seen had prepared me for the sight of Plymouth," wrote a US war correspondent after visiting the city which had been pounded by German bombs throughout March and April 1941. Nearly a thousand were killed in the raids and 40,000 made homeless.*

AIR RAIDS

When the ululating siren sounded, as it did night after night, it was a warning that an air raid was imminent and people should seek shelter. If it was a night raid, householders might go down to their cellar or basement, if they had one. Alternatively, if they had a corrugated-steel Anderson shelter dug into the garden, they might trail down there with blankets and pillows and settle down on a makeshift bunk for the night. If they had neither, they might huddle in an under-stairs cupboard or even under the kitchen table. Or they might decide, in the parlance of the time, that if a bomb had your name on it, that would be that anyway, and you might as well spend the night in your own bed.

Towards the end of the Blitz, Morrison shelters (named after the Home Secretary, Herbert Morrison) became available for flat dwellers or for those who had neither cellars nor garden shelters. The Morrison shelter had a heavy steel top on what was essentially a mesh cage, and offered protection against falling debris in the event of a raid.

Others with no choice of air-raid shelter at home, or feeling that there was safety in numbers, would make for a public shelter. This might be a basement in a civic building, requisitioned space in an office, or a purpose-built public street shelter. There were never enough of the last-named, and many were very unsatisfactory. This was partly due to wrangling between government and local authorities about who should pay for shelter provision, and partly because, when the raids did start, they often lasted all night rather than being short and intense, as had been expected. Consequently, public shelters had been built without sanitary facilities or anywhere to sit down. And they did not, on the whole, inspire public confidence either. Many had been built cheaply and in haste, and

over 5,000 shelters in London alone were found to be in danger of collapse soon after being built.

All over the country, people sheltered from air raids in the nearest "safe" place: under railway bridges, in the Mersey Tunnel or in the Chislehurst Caves in Kent. At first, the government was reluctant to build deep shelters, largely due to cost but also because it was feared that people might develop a shelter mentality and refuse to come up again even when the immediate danger was deemed to be past.

These reasons, plus a reluctance to encourage large numbers of people to congregate, allied to the need to keep transport running efficiently, caused the Home Secretary to refuse to allow the London Underground to be used for shelter. But as soon as the Blitz began, Londoners ignored the ban and swarmed into the Underground; the Home Secretary had little option but to admit a *fait accompli*. As many as 177,000 people were regularly spending the night down in Tube stations during the height of the Blitz – though even this large number was just 4 per cent of those living in central London. Gradually, the appalling conditions were improved: regular cleaning, better lighting, sanitary facilities, bunks and canteens were introduced, and entertainment laid on. But nowhere was "safe" in the event of a direct hit – at least 55 people were killed at Bank when a bomb crashed through the booking hall and 64 at Balham when the tunnel flooded with water, sewage and silt after a bomb in the High Street broke into the tunnel.

RIGHT *ARP wardens on duty in west London. Some are carrying axes or crowbars to help them break into unoccupied premises if necessary during an air raid.*

BELOW *An ARP warden's tin hat.*

ABOVE *On 20 September 1940 the superfluous Aldwych section of the Piccadilly line was closed and prepared as a public underground shelter. The track was covered over with sleepers, bunks and improved lavatory facilities installed, a library set up, and several thousand Londoners made it their night-time home during the Blitz.*

It was the role of tin-hatted ARP wardens to patrol the streets during a raid. ARP wardens were local men and women who knew the names of the residents in their sector, which ones went to which shelter, the whereabouts of the old and infirm, where the fire hydrants were and other vital information. If there was an "incident", as a bomb falling was called, the nearest warden would assess what help was needed, ring the control centre – if the lines weren't down – with a report, and then try to assist by controlling small fires, giving first aid and helping those who had been bombed out to the nearest rest centre.

If the incident was a major one, the fire services and Heavy Rescue squad would arrive, and would attempt to lift debris and fallen masonry in order to reach anyone who was trapped underneath. A first-aid (or stretcher) party would deal with minor injuries on the spot, and transport casualties either to first-aid posts or, if the injuries were more serious, to hospital. The ARP warden would make sure bombed premises were not looted; later, mortuary vans would arrive to take away the bodies of anyone killed in the "incident".

ANDERSON SHELTERS

Anderson shelters, named after the Home Secretary at the time, Sir John Anderson, were masterpieces of simple engineering, consisting of two steel plates bolted at the top to form an arch. Official instructions indicated a hole 1m 22cm (4ft) deep should be dug to take the standard 1m 96cm (6ft 6in)-long shelter. Soil was heaped on top for further protection and most people fashioned bunks or seats inside to sit out a raid. Flooding was always a problem, as were lack of lighting and heating – and noise. The shelters were distributed free to anyone earning less than £250 a year; by September 1940 nearly a quarter of a million were in place, mostly in back yards or gardens.

LEFT *The furniture of war. A housewife hanging her washing out in the back garden next to a corrugated-iron Anderson shelter protected by a layer of soil.*

THE MINISTRY OF INFORMATION

The Second World War was a "People's War", involving the entire civilian population from the start. To fight this "People's War" successfully, people would be required to make huge sacrifices, they would be regulated and directed in unprecedented ways, and would suffer danger and deprivation. Thus the morale of the nation would be of the utmost importance in the successful prosecution of the war: if morale collapsed, then Britain's leaders would have little choice but to sue for peace. How was the nation to be kept "on side" in the months, perhaps years, before Britain had a military victory (not until November 1942 at El Alamein in North Africa, in fact – although Wavell's desert offensive and conquest of the Italian African Empire did bring victories in early 1941, these were against Mussolini, not Hitler) and when rationing, shortages and long working hours had begun to seem a permanent way of life?

Monitoring and reporting on morale was one of the key functions of the Ministry of Information (MoI), established on the outbreak of war. The MoI grew rapidly, so that soon it had a reputed 999 people working for it, including the poet John Betjeman, the urbane cartoonist and writer Osbert Lancaster and a handful of women, including P. L. Travers, the creator of "Mary Poppins". It was housed in the neo-Brutalist building of the University of London's Senate House and its role was, from the start, ambiguous. Its first three ministers, Lord Macmillan, Sir John Reith (the stern moral conscience of the BBC) and Duff Cooper, were not a success, alienating both press and public in turn. But Churchill's protégé and confidant Brendan Bracken, who was appointed in June 1941, was.

Bracken was rightly scornful of his predecessors' attempts to mobilize the wartime spirit of the British people with a series of deeply condescending posters which patronized and irritated in equal measure. In his eyes, morale was maintained not by exhortation but by keeping the public as fully informed as was possible in wartime conditions.

As well as generating encouragement and information, the MoI was also charged with protecting national security by controlling the news and information that appeared in newspapers, magazines and films, and on the radio. The press was assured that, since Britain was engaged in a war with a totalitarian state for the freedom of democracy, there would be no unnecessary gags put on the press: only military matters and information that could be shown to be of use to the enemy would be censored.

Under Emergency Powers legislation, newspaper publishers, like everyone else, were prohibited from obtaining or passing on any information that might be useful to the enemy, such as weather forecasts or any mention of the weather for the next ten

LEFT *One of the early inept and patronizing posters put out by the Ministry of Information. Removing the "Y" to make "Your" into "Our" would have made all the difference.*

BELOW *Brendan Bracken (centre), the most effective of the wartime Ministers of Information, holding a joint press conference with the US Secretary of the Treasury, Henry Morgenthau Jr, who was responsible for financing the American war effort.*

YOUR COURAGE
YOUR CHEERFULNESS
YOUR RESOLUTION
WILL BRING
US VICTORY

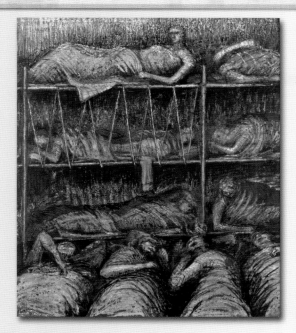

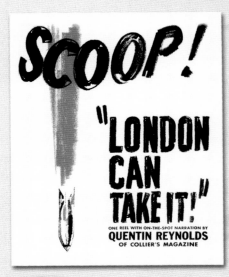

RIGHT *The poster for Humphrey Jennings and Harry Watt's film* London Can Take It! *(1940), made to bring the reality of the Blitz to American audiences. The US journalist Quentin Reynolds, a war correspondent in Britain, provided the commentary.*

BELOW *Fougasse (real name Kenneth Bird, Art Editor of Punch) designed several witty and sophisticated posters for the Ministry of Information's "Careless Talk" campaign, aimed at foiling spies and "fifth columnists".*

WAR ARTISTS

Anxious to "keep artists in work on any pretext, and, as far as possible, prevent them from being killed", Sir Kenneth Clark, then director of the National Gallery, revived a First World War scheme commissioning artists to paint the scenes of war. He gave it the new title of the War Artists' Advisory Committee. But the Second World War was a different sort of war from the First, and answering the "what did it look like?" question of future generations meant depicting not only battlefield scenes but also the Underground as a bomb shelter, women canning surplus produce, and people winching barrage balloons.

ABOVE Shelter scene: Bunks and Sleepers, *a 1941 sketch by Henry Moore, an official war artist, of Londoners sleeping in the Underground, which owes much to the sinuous reclining shapes of his sculptures.*

spreading rumours, absenteeism and complaining about those in authority, whereas volunteering, cheerfulness, co-operation and high productivity represented high morale.

Contributing to the nation's feeling of being kept informed was the MoI's film unit, which built on the already distinguished British documentary film industry associated with the name of John Grierson. During the war, 1,887 films were made under the auspices of the MoI, on such diverse subjects as composting, blood transfusions and "Get the Coke [a by-product of coal] Habit". Although by no means all were universally popular with the audiences who saw them at cinemas, church halls or factories, some, such as Humphrey Jennings's *Listen to Britain* and *Fires Were Started*, remain among the finest evocations of the wartime years.

days. But they also had a duty to keep the public informed. Since such distinctions were not simple to decide, the Ministry soon earned the soubriquet "Ministry of Disinformation" and the radio comedy show *ITMA* satirized it as the "Ministry of Aggravation and Mysteries", which did not always seem all that far from the mark. The system was voluntary and depended on editors accepting that the censor's decisions were reasonable. Even so, in the early days of the war before some sort of "case law" was established, there were many conundrums, such as whether it was possible to mention that the employees of Battersea Power Station were to play a football match, since that could draw it to the attention of German bombers. Though it seems unlikely that the Luftwaffe had failed to notice the power station.

It was equally hard to decide what exactly "morale" was. The best working definition seemed to be that offered by the MoI's Director of Home Intelligence: morale must "ultimately be measured not by what a person thinks or says, but what he does and how he does it". Low morale might include grumbling,

TAKING THE WAR TO GERMANY

"When I look round to see how we can win this war there is only one sure path… and that is an absolutely devastating, exterminating attack by very heavy bombers from this country upon the Nazi homeland," wrote Winston Churchill in July 1940. By then, Hitler's forces controlled Europe from Northern Norway to the French–Spanish border and the only way of taking the fight to Germany was by bombing from the air.

During the so-called "phoney war", the RAF had been reluctant to provoke German bombing raids. Bomber Command's capability for offensive attack was still limited – its planes were slow and had primitive navigational aids. Raids had therefore largely been confined to dropping propaganda leaflets on Germany by night; any daylight excursions had resulted in heavy losses of men and aircraft.

The German attack on Rotterdam on 14 May 1940 changed British policy. Although it was still a relatively small and under-equipped force, Bomber Command was ordered to attack Germany itself, aiming specifically at airfields, oil refineries, transport networks and factories believed to be engaged in war production.

On 24 August 1940, the first German bombs fell on central London; the next night Bomber Command attacked Berlin. Churchill, anxious to show that the Germans were "getting as good as they were giving", urged a campaign of "area bombing" of German towns and cities "for their intrinsic industrial and psychological value" rather than for their strategic importance. He

was supported by much of the British press in this. The war was to be taken to the German people as the Germans were taking it to the British. "Oil and Morale" were to be the twin targets for the next year or so, with oil taking priority, until this was seen to be ineffective. In March 1941 Bomber Command was switched to prioritize attacking German U-boats in the Atlantic, a move dictated by the heavy toll they were taking on Allied shipping.

In August 1941, a damning report commissioned by Lord Cherwell, Churchill's scientific advisor, revealed that when flying at night with primitive navigation aids, just 30 per cent of bombers found their way to within five miles of specific targets. Hundreds of airmen had died in the effort, to little effect other than "the annoyance of the enemy", in Churchill's words. Since hitting specific targets was so problematic, precision raids would only be carried

BELOW *Operation THUNDERCLAP brought death and destruction to Hamburg over ten nights starting on 24–25 July 1943. It is estimated that more that 50,000 were killed in the conflagration and as many injured.*

ABOVE *A Lancaster bomber on a raid on Hamburg. More than 6,000 acres of the city were razed in the concerted saturation bombing that started in July 1943.*

out in particular circumstances with favourable conditions. Area bombing would be the first priority – but Bomber Command needed to be upgraded if it was to have any real effect on Germany.

Air Marshal "Bomber" Harris was appointed as Commander of Bomber Command in February 1942, and four-engined Lancaster bombers with more sophisticated navigational aids started to come into operation. Directive 22, issued on 14 February 1942, had ordered that "the primary object of your [Bomber Command's] operations should now be focused on the morale of the enemy civilian population and in particular of the industrial workers…". A primary object of what Cherwell described as a "de-housing policy" was the houses of German industrial workers, deemed legitimate targets because if workers had nowhere to live they could not work. On 30–31 May 1942 came the first 1,000-bomber raid on Cologne. "One bomb every 6 seconds, 3,000 tons in 90 minutes… Let Him Have it right on the chin… Germans squeal havoc, misery," the headlines of the *Daily Express* trumpeted.

British Bombers now attack Germany a thousand at a time!

Aided by the formation of a "pathfinder" group that guided planes to their targets by the use of coloured flares, Bomber Command pounded Germany night after night for three and a half years, aiming at industrial targets, railways, roads and dams, dropping mines to blow up ships and submarines and, after 1944, aiming at the launching pads of the deadly V-1 "secret" weapons in northern France. At the same time, bombing raids on the German people continued. In July and August 1943, four major raids on Hamburg caused a conflagration in which the city was devastated and more than 50,000 people were killed.

The heaviest "saturation bombing" of Germany came in the final six months of the war, when RAF and USAAF bombers laid waste to Duisberg, most of the industrial cities of the Ruhr and Dresden. Perhaps as many as 40,000 people were incinerated in the fires that razed Dresden on 13–14 February 1945. Despite Churchill's late doubts on both the morality and the effectiveness of the bombing campaign, RAF Bomber Command continued to attack targets in Germany up until the first week of May 1945. The bombing offensive cost the lives of over 55,000 aircrew and 8,000 aircraft. Bomber Command's final sorties were to drop food supplies to the starving populations of Holland and Belgium and to repatriate British and Commonwealth POWs from camps in Europe.

BELOW *A Handley Page Halifax of No. 6 Bomber Command during a daylight raid on an oil refinery in the Ruhr in October 1944.*

FAR LEFT *A poster referring to the 1,000-bomber raids, in which 1,000 aircraft attacked German cities at the same time. The intention of the raids was to break German morale. The first such raid was on Cologne on 30–31 May 1942, when 600 acres of the city were razed.*

DRESDEN

"How many died? Who knows the number?" reads the plaque in Dresden's memorial cemetery. The raids on Dresden on 13–14 February 1945 unleashed 4,500 tons of bombs on the inadequately defended city; maybe 25,000, more likely 50,000 and possibly up to 70,000, died in the conflagration, some of them Jews working as forced labour and refugees fleeing the advancing Red Army. Dresden has become synonymous with the sickening futility of war, the ultimate indictment of area bombardment and the emerging power politics of post-war Europe in which East would vie with West for hegemony.

LEFT *"It seems to me", Churchill wrote in a memo on 28 March 1945 a few weeks after the bombing of Dresden, "that the moment has come when the question of bombing German cities… should be reviewed…".*

WARTIME INTELLIGENCE

Security in wartime was the responsibility of MI5 and MI6, two parallel bodies established before the First World War. When war broke out in 1939, MI5 was responsible, under the auspices of the Home Office, for counter-espionage in the UK and in the countries of the Empire (in wartime, responsibilities abroad had to be delegated to local bodies). MI6, which was responsible for military espionage abroad, was transformed into the Special Intelligence Services (SIS) attached to the Foreign Office. It included a special "Section D" that specialized in subversion and sabotage and also briefly employed the Cold War spy Guy Burgess, until he was sacked for incompetence.

MI5's responsibility for security in Britain involved it throughout the war in tensions between the liberty of the individual and the security of the state. Members of the British Union of Fascists and National Socialists, the Communist Party of Great Britain and any other person or organization that might be thought to be a threat to Britain's security came under close surveillance. In the summer of 1940, MI5 was overwhelmed by the "fifth columnist" scare, when reports flooded in from the public denouncing suspect "alien activities", rarely with hard evidence to back their suspicions.

MI5's greatest wartime success was running "double agents" through the XX committee. This was set up in January 1941 to operate the "double-cross system" by "turning" *Abwehr* (the German military intelligence and counter-intelligence service) agents as they arrived in the UK (usually by parachute) and were captured or gave themselves up. These agents were interrogated about German plans, then action was taken based on this information. Later, MI5 used double agents to deceive Germany about Allied intentions and resources. By mid-1942, MI5 was working to feed false information to the Germans about the timing and location of the Normandy landings.

MI6 had been starved of resources in the inter-war years and its notable deficiencies early in the war meant that the service's morale was at a low ebb after its failure to anticipate both Hitler's invasion of Norway in April 1940 and Operation BARBAROSSA, the invasion of the USSR, in June 1941. In July 1940, Churchill decided to incorporate Section D into the newly established Special Operations Executive (SOE), which was designed to promote subversive warfare in enemy-occupied territory by providing money, clothing, forged documents, weapons and training to resistance fighters and those acting as wireless operators as well as sabotaging war production industries, transport and more. This merger enabled British intelligence to make a real contribution to the underground war against the Third Reich.

Vital to knowing the enemy's intentions was the ability to intercept wireless transmissions between enemy commanders and those in the field. The Government Code and Cypher School (GC&CS) had moved to Bletchley Park, a mansion in Buckinghamshire, just before the outbreak of war. Here, in concrete huts, known for security reasons only by a number, worked initially 100 and, by January 1945, 9,000 men and

ALAN TURING (1912–54)

One of the team of brilliant thinkers at Bletchley Park, the mathematician and logician Alan Mathison Turing, in conjunction with another Cambridge mathematician, W. G. Welshman, developed the Bombe electromechanical machine that was to prove crucial during the Battle of the Atlantic. Based on an earlier Polish device called Bomba, the Bombe was capable of breaking into any of the early Enigma messages using as a "crib" a section of matching plain text and cipher text. The first Bombe was installed in March 1940: by the end of the war over 200 were in operation.

RIGHT *A German Enigma machine. Although the Germans modified Enigma throughout the war, the gifted team of code-breakers at Bletchley Park managed to keep pace with the changes and gather a wealth of essential intelligence about German plans.*

women. These individuals were intent on "breaking the code" of German messages, summarizing and dispatching their contents, evaluating the importance of the intelligence gathered and indexing everything so that the "big picture" of enemy action and intentions could be assembled.

The "Y" service, a chain of wireless intercept stations across Britain and in several overseas countries, listened in to enemy radio messages, as did thousands of wireless operators, both civilian and military. These messages were relayed to "Station X" at Bletchley Park. The messages had been converted into a series of cyphers or a code, and they had to be painstakingly decrypted or decoded and fitted together with various other pieces of information, like some giant jigsaw puzzle, to reveal enemy movements.

It was immensely demanding work. German codes, which were encrypted on an Enigma cypher machine, were changed every 24 hours at midnight, so cracking the 150 million million million possible settings was a round-the-clock, day-in-day-out operation employing the keenest mathematical, logical – and imaginative – abilities. And the work was top secret. The code breakers worked on their assigned task, were never told how it might relate to anything else, and were sworn to secrecy about the work they were doing.

To Churchill, the information received from the code-breakers at Bletchley was like "golden eggs" and he commended the "geese" that "laid" them for "never cackling". They were so circumspect that

the existence of ULTRA, the code-name used for the intelligence derived from the decryption of important enemy cyphers, which proved decisive at the Battle of Matapan in 1941, the Battle of Alam el Halfa in 1942 and the sinking of the *Scharnhorst* in December 1943, among others, was not revealed until the 1970s.

ABOVE *Bletchley Park was about to be demolished when, needing a safe home with excellent transport links for its code-breaking work, MI6 took over the mansion, code-naming it "Station X" for the duration.*

LEFT *A sketch of work at Gayhurst Manor, one of the several out-stations near to Bletchley Park where the Bombes, decyphering devices, were housed.*

BELOW *Hut 3 hard at work: over the course of the war as many as 12,000 people – men and women, military personnel and civilians – worked at Bletchley Park. Wooden huts were erected to accommodate the overflow.*

MANPOWER SHORTAGES

During 1941 the realities of war hit home hard. It was a grim year. The Battle of the Atlantic was going so badly, with 412 Allied and neutral ships lost at sea between March and May, that Churchill ordered that shipping losses should no longer be reported in the press; the fighting in the Western Desert was inconclusive after Wavell's early successes; and food rations were lower than at any time during the war. Furthermore, there was an acute production crisis on the Home Front.

Since there had still been over a million unemployed in Britain in May 1940, it had been assumed that there would be plenty of spare labour to staff the expanding war industries; Ernest Bevin, the Minister of Labour, believed in "voluntaryism", as he called it. Then came a sobering report in December 1940 from the Manpower Requirements Committee chaired by Sir William Beveridge, which showed that the armed services and Civil Defence needed a further 1,750,000 men and 84,000 women. The only way to make up the shortfall would be to call up around half a million men then in reserved occupations into the munitions work. However, there was no point in expanding the armed forces if they did not have sufficient equipment to fight with. To ensure the supply of tanks, planes, lorries and weapons, another 1.5 million workers were needed to supplement the 3.5 million already working in the munitions industries.

The reserved occupation scheme was overhauled to release more younger men for the Forces and since the designation "skilled engineer" could cover a man working in a toy factory providing that he was over a certain age, the categories were re-examined. It was decided that women, many of whom seemed reluctant to accept the government's blandishments to "Come into the Factories", would have to be compelled to provide half the number needed in munitions. Another 750,000 would be required in other industries to replace the men who had been

RIGHT *The War Artists' Advisory Committee sent the painter Stanley Spencer to record shipbuilding on the Clyde, where vessels were being turned out at rapid speed to replace those lost in the Battle of the Atlantic.*

ABOVE *Britain never stood alone: Empire and Commonwealth workers arrived to help win the war. Here technicians from India construct aircraft at the Government Training Centre at Letchworth, Hertfordshire in 1941.*

ERNEST BEVIN (1881–1951)

Known in the 1920s as the "Docker's KC [King's Counsel]" because of his negotiating skills, Ernest Bevin actually left school at the aged of 11. In May 1940, as General Secretary of Britain's biggest union, the Transport & General Workers' Union, with upwards of 650,000 members, Bevin was, in Churchill's eyes, the obvious choice to join the War Cabinet as Minister of Labour and National Service. Although he preferred voluntary measures, Bevin was prepared to use compulsion to increase war production, while maximizing the opportunities for increased job security and improved working conditions in return for an "all out effort" in a total war.

LEFT *"I believe it is a social obligation to defend your homeland," claimed Ernest Bevin, and his contribution to the war effort was to mobilize Britain's labour force.*

called up into the Forces or transferred to munitions work.

The wartime workplace was tightly regulated by the first Essential Work Order of March 1941. Bevin had decreed that certain privately owned factories were doing "national work" which was either essential to the war effort or to the life of the community. The Essential Work Order meant that the 4.5 million workers in such factories could neither leave nor be sacked without the permission of the local National Service Office, except in the case of gross misconduct. Mechanisms were set up for trade unions to secure adequate wages for their workers and to negotiate industrial disputes. This was because, despite strikes having been declared illegal in 1940, over a million working days had been lost due to strike action in 1941; by 1942, the figure exceeded the pre-war level.

The engineering and aircraft industries were the first to come under the scope of these new provisions, which were soon extended to shipbuilding, railways and coal mining. Shipbuilding had suffered high levels of unemployment in the depression of the 1930s, but the demands of war had boosted the need for ships and full employment was resumed.

It was a different picture in coal mining. Coal was the lifeblood of Britain's war industries, but it had serious labour problems, which

had come to a head in the General Strike of 1926, and the war offered young men a way out of the troubled industry. After the fall of France, coal lost its main export market and by 1943 there was an ageing workforce of only 710,000 men working down the mines. An additional 20,000 were needed by the end of the year but volunteers were not forthcoming. The answer, again, was found in compulsion. The "Bevin Boys Scheme" meant that all men of 25 and under who had not yet enlisted or had not yet reached call-up age would, in effect, enter a lottery and 10 per cent would be selected by ballot to go down the mines. It was not a popular move. Forty per cent of those selected objected, but only 466 out of 8,619 had their appeals allowed; eventually, 147 were sent to prison for refusing to obey their Direction.

While the Bevin Boys scheme was no solution to the long-term problems in the coal mining industry (which would be nationalized after the war, in 1947), the 21,800 men who served as "Bevin Boys", plus the 16,000 optants (who had opted for coal mining when called up for the Forces) proved to be a short-term emergency answer to a wartime crisis.

RIGHT *Conscript "Bevin Boys" being trained by a regular miner at a Kent coalfield near Canterbury in October 1944.*

WOMEN ON THE FRONT LINE

Women were on the Front Line even before the official declaration of war. After blackout regulations came into effect on 1 September 1939, it usually fell to housewives to search out fast-disappearing black material in the shops, paste tape across the windows of their houses as protection against bomb blasts, decide where the family would shelter when the raids came and then make the chosen space as comfortable as possible in the circumstances. Then there was anxiety about evacuation for mothers in cities, or the added responsibility of caring for an evacuee for those in supposedly "safe" areas.

The introduction of food rationing in January 1940 meant further headaches. As the war dragged on, daily life became harder for those running a home, with queuing and shortages the norm, so that considerable ingenuity was needed to feed a family on whatever could be obtained. When clothes went "on the ration" in June 1941, the struggle to clothe the family and the need to "make do and mend" made yet more work. And there were few treats anymore – silk stockings were almost unobtainable and cosmetics scarce – unless you happened to have a "black market" contact.

But it wasn't just in the home that women contributed to the nation's war effort. From the start, many young women volunteered for the women's services, the ATS, the WRNS or the WAAF. Others opted for a wartime life on the land – and that could be a hard, if enjoyable, experience, out in all weathers and certainly not all feeding baby lambs in the sunshine as the recruiting posters for the Women's Land Army (WLA) suggested – or as "Lumber Jills" or "Polecats" in the Timber Corps. Women "manned" anti-aircraft posts despite initial male prejudice, hoisted 500-lb hydrogen-filled barrage balloons aloft to deter enemy aircraft and worked as ARP wardens, ambulance drivers, auxiliary police women and in the Women's Auxiliary Fire Service. Others chose to nurse, work in transport on the railways, buses or even barges, or go into war production factories and contribute to the war effort that way.

But volunteers were not enough. By 1941 the acute manpower crisis both in the armed forces and in the factories made it clear that women were going to have to make up the shortfall. The terms of the National Service (No 2) Act that became law on 18 December 1941 meant that Britain was the first nation in the world in modern times to conscript

ABOVE *Members of the ATS operating a night-time range finder on an Anti-Aircraft "Ack Ack" site in December 1942. The women, in the words of their C-in-C, "lived like men, fought their fights like men and, alas, some of them died like men".*

LEFT *No. 230873 Second Subaltern Elizabeth Alexandra Mary Windsor, the present Queen, a new recruit to the ATS in February 1945.*

women. Single women and childless widows between the ages of 20 and 30 were liable for war work (the age was lowered to 19 in 1943) and could, in theory, elect either to join one of the women's auxiliary services or to be directed into industry or

THE WVS

The original purpose of the Women's Voluntary Service (WVS), founded in 1938, had been to recruit women into ARP work, but when war came, its remit widened beyond any previously imagined horizon, in line with its motto "The WVS Never Says No". At its peak there were 1.3 million "women in green" escorting evacuees, helping refugees, mending soldiers' socks, making camouflage nets, lending out wedding dresses, running mobile canteens for shelterers and air-raid victims, and acting as information points after a major bomb incident.

LEFT *Members of the WVS "shopping squad" from Hounslow in West London in March 1941. The women would take orders at factories, cycle round the shops and deliver the goods to the doorsteps of women working in war factories who did not have time to shop for their families themselves.*

Civil Defence. In practice, this usually meant the ATS or munitions factories where labour shortages were most acute. By the end of the war, 125,000 recruits had been called up into the women's auxiliary services to join the larger number who had volunteered.

But it wasn't just these "mobile" women who were pressed into service. Pregnant women, those with a child under 14 years living at home, or with heavy domestic responsibilities such as caring for an elderly relative (a father, that is; mothers didn't count) would not be directed into war work – although, of course, they could volunteer for the WVS or other organizations, and many did. But all other married women under the age of 50 were obliged to register with their local labour exchange. Depending on a woman's circumstances, she could be directed into war work locally.

By the end of 1942 10 million women aged between 19 and 50 were registered for war work. Seven and a half million were in full-time paid work and around 380,000 were part-timers (which could mean 30 hours a week). There were nearly half a million women in the armed forces and, by June 1942, 76,800 women in Civil Defence. For the first time in their lives many married women worked outside the home just when work in the home was more arduous.

Women might be doing a "man's job" in wartime, as the propaganda put it, but they were doing it for less pay, often with less than adequate nursery provision for their children, and in the knowledge that when the men came back from war, they would be entitled to reclaim their jobs from Britain's army of women wartime workers.

ABOVE *"A woman cannot be expected to pull her weight in a factory if she is worrying about her children all day." By July 1943 there were 1,245 government-sponsored nurseries for mothers working in wartime production. Painting by Elsie Dalton Hewland.*

LEFT *While some industries had a tradition of employing women and war led to their – sometimes grudging – acceptance, much opposition was faced in heavy industries such as ship building. By 1943 women still only constituted nine per cent of the workforce, though once agreements with the unions had been worked out, they were able to make a contribution. Here, women give the order for steel girders to be lifted in a ship yard.*

"FOR THE DURATION": SHORTAGES

Things that in peacetime had been an irritation could become a minor tragedy in wartime. If a housewife broke a pie dish, for example, with so many factories turned over to war production, the chance of finding another one in the shops was close to zero. By war's end, many families drank out of handleless cups and ate from chipped plates that could not be replaced. In their patriotic response to the Minister of Aircraft Production's request, housewives had eagerly volunteered their aluminium saucepans, kettles, colanders and fish slices supposedly to make Spitfires, only to bitterly regret it now that these could no longer be bought and it was clear that there had been plenty of other sources of metal apart from precious kitchen utensils.

Nevertheless, it was a shock when clothes rationing was announced on Whit Sunday, 1 June 1941, in order "to provide fair distribution of available supplies". The intention was also to limit consumer spending and release workers and factory space for war production. As with food, clothes would require coupons as well as money; at first, margarine coupons had to be used, as secrecy demanded that clothing coupons could not be distributed in advance.

RIGHT WVS Clothing Exchange (1943) by Evelyn Gibbs. Those who had lost their possessions in air raids were able to reclothe their children thanks to the WVS.

At the outset of clothes rationing, everyone received 66 coupons a year, which was calculated to provide roughly two-thirds of the amount of clothing bought by an individual before the war. This allocation dropped to 40 coupons in 1943, increased to 60 in 1942 and became 48 in 1944. A man could just about clothe himself on his allocation: a three-piece suit required 26 coupons, a shirt five, vest and pants eight, socks three, shoes seven and a tie one, which left 16 coupons for pyjamas, a dressing gown and maybe some handkerchiefs (one coupon for two).

Women would need 14 coupons for a coat or suit over 28 inches long (11 if it were under 28 inches), but only nine for an unlined mackintosh. A woollen dress was 11 coupons and a rayon or cotton one seven; a pair of stockings needed two coupons (which was soon a privation) and a bra or suspender belt one each. Hats did not require coupons.

Clothes for children under four did not require coupons until August, and since they used less material they "cost" fewer coupons. But because children outgrew their clothes as well as wearing them out, from 1942 each child received an extra

"MAKE DO AND MEND"

Women's magazines told their readers that it was "patriotic to be shabby", but with clothes rationing and shortages, there was not much choice in the matter. Advice came from every side on how to unravel worn jumpers and knit them into something new, cut the sleeves out of coats to make jerkins, make blankets and even bedspreads into coats, cut up adult clothes for children and children's for babies. The Board of Trade ran a "Make Do and Mend" campaign full of handy hints such as reinforcing new socks and stockings before wearing them and other such time-consuming wheezes.

ABOVE *During the war, paper shortages meant that the circulation of magazines was restricted and they also shrunk in size, but women found the wartime recipes and hints in* Housewife *and similar publications invaluable in their changed lives.*

BELOW *A woman buying underwear at Woolworths the week that clothes rationing was introduced. She would have needed three coupons each for vests and knickers – plus the purchase price.*

RIGHT With growing children, there never seemed enough coupons to go round, so the WVS set up clothing exchange depots where outgrown clothes in good condition could be bartered for the next size up.

BELOW Clothing coupon books, required for buying almost all articles of clothing – except hats – after June 1941. Clothes ration books were not issued in June 1941 and margarine coupons had to be used instead.

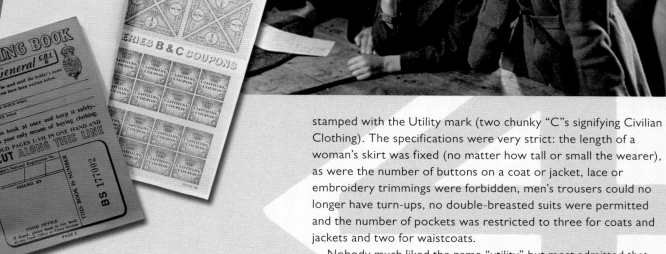

ten coupons, with adolescents and "outsize" children (who had to be weighed and measured annually to make sure) receiving 20. Pregnant women were allowed extra coupons to buy maternity clothes and a layette for the baby.

Churchill had been dubious about rationing clothes, fearing it would be a deprivation too far, and although at first most people were fairly stoical about it, they found it an increasing struggle to clothe themselves on the allotted amount. As usual, the less well off, who did not have a capacious pre-rationing wardrobe, and could only afford cheaper clothes that did not last, suffered more. There were also endless complaints that children needed a larger allocation, especially for shoes, and about the number of coupons required for babies' nappies (24 per packet).

"Utility" is now a word that is indelibly linked to wartime, the epitome of dreary regulation. But when the first utility clothes were shown to the press in September 1942, the high-fashion magazine *Vogue* welcomed the scheme as "an outstanding idea of advanced democracy". Intent on ensuring that an adequate number of good-quality clothes were produced at a reasonable price (clothes prices had risen by nearly 100 per cent since the start of the war), the Board of Trade selected a number of outfits designed by top couturiers to be mass-produced. To qualify, the clothes had to be made from specified "Utility" fabrics and

stamped with the Utility mark (two chunky "C"s signifying Civilian Clothing). The specifications were very strict: the length of a woman's skirt was fixed (no matter how tall or small the wearer), as were the number of buttons on a coat or jacket, lace or embroidery trimmings were forbidden, men's trousers could no longer have turn-ups, no double-breasted suits were permitted and the number of pockets was restricted to three for coats and jackets and two for waistcoats.

Nobody much liked the name "utility" but most admitted that the quality and range of clothes were surprisingly good – and that the pared-down look chimed well with the "roll up your sleeves" mood of wartime.

RIGHT A woman and two girls model utility underwear in 1943: plain and practical with no additional frills or flounces, it conformed to government "CC41" standards.

"OVER HERE"— GIS COME TO BRITAIN

On the "day of infamy", 7 December 1941, when Japan bombed the US fleet at Pearl Harbor, Hawaii, Winston Churchill knew that at last "the US was in the war... after 17 months of lonely fighting... [Britain] had won the war... Once again... we should emerge, however mauled and mutilated, safe and victorious...." In 1939 some people in America viewed the war as yet another struggle in Europe's endless civil war. Gradually, President Franklin D. Roosevelt had managed to move his country towards Britain's side, a move that culminated in the introduction of Lend Lease in March 1941, by which America would become "the great arsenal for democracy".

Churchill set sail for America straight after Pearl Harbor. In Washington, on New Year's Day 1942, the British Prime Minister and the US President signed an agreement under which American GIs (GI stood for General Issue, which was stamped on equipment and became a nickname for American soldiers in World War II) would be sent to Britain both to help defend the UK against possible invasion and to prepare for the Allied fight back, the invasion of "Fortress Europe" and the defeat of Hitler.

The first GIs arrived in Belfast on 26 January 1942. Gradually, US troops would take over a triangle of Britain stretching from their ports of entry on the west coast down to Hampshire and Cornwall, while British and Canadian forces were concentrated in the south-east. This was part of Operation BOLERO, the code-name for the build-up of US troops in Britain that would rise to a crescendo with the invasion of Europe. The first GIs had come to build airfields in East Anglia ready for the USAAF bombers that were to join the RAF in what would become almost round-the-clock raids on Germany and occupied Europe. By the end of 1944, nearly all the 426,000 US airmen in Britain were stationed in Norfolk and Suffolk. A hundred thousand acres of farmland in Norfolk alone had been requisitioned, and the whole of East Anglia had become a mosaic of airfields, with one roughly every eight miles.

Ground forces did not begin to arrive in large numbers until the autumn of 1943, so that there were fewer than a quarter of a million GIs stationed in the UK at the end of 1942. By May 1944, an invasion force of 1.5 million combat and service troops, plus all their equipment, was stationed in a country one-third the size of Texas.

ABOVE *The US President Franklin D. Roosevelt and the British Prime Minister Winston S. Churchill in conversation aboard HMS* Prince of Wales *off the coast of Newfoundland in August 1941 when the US was still maintaining its position of benevolent neutrality.*

BELOW *Flying officers scramble to their plane in Essex in August 1942. Their "Eagle" squadron was formed from American volunteers as part of RAF Fighter Command during the Battle of Britain when the US was neutral. It was not operational until February 1941.*

The impact was overwhelming; the GIs were "Over-fed, Over-paid, Over-sexed and Over Here" in the view of most British soldiers. Overpaid by British standards certainly, particularly in the lower ranks, since a British private was paid 14 shillings (70p) a week as compared to his US counterpart's weekly wage of £3 8s 9d. (£3.44). *A Short Guide to Britain*, which was issued to all US troops, warned that "The British 'Tommy' is apt to be specially touchy about the difference between his wages and yours. Keep this in mind…". But the GIs, many of them young conscripts, far from home, didn't always, as they splashed money around, drinking pubs dry of weak, warm beer and giving British girls a good time – which is what led to the "over-sexed" charge.

"Having a Yank" was something that many British girls yearned for. This was because it could mean lavish gifts of things that were virtually unobtainable in wartime Britain, such as nylon stockings, silk scarves and chocolates, as well as frequent dances at a US base or GI-only club such as the Rainbow Corner in Piccadilly, jitterbugging and lindy hopping to "swing" bands. It also meant an alarming rise in VD rates, more illegitimate babies, taunts of being

LEFT *The cover to the GIs' Guide to Britain.*

a "spam bag", and heartbreak. But some 70,000 British women did marry their "Yank" and after the war sailed to a new life "over there".

"Over-fed" could be turned to British advantage. Children found many GIs generous in dispensing sweets, comics and chewing gum. Housewives, meanwhile, who were encouraged to invite a GI to tea to make him feel at home, and to foster good Anglo–American relations, were rewarded with such peacetime delicacies as tinned peaches, tinned ham, cigarettes (and bourbon for father), brought from the Post Exchange, or PX for short (the American equivalent of the British forces' canteen or NAAFI).

"Over Here" meant a sometimes uneasy co-operation between British forces and 1.5 million men (and a few women) that war had brought more than 6,000 miles to Britain, and who knew that their only way home was via victory in Europe.

BLACK GIS

The US Army that came to Britain was segregated. Almost all black GIs were trained for non-combatant tasks until heavy losses in the fighting across France after D-Day meant more were recruited for battle. Many black GIs were employed in building runways in East Anglia for the USAAF and acting as supply staff, ground crew and labourers. Black GIs were obliged to spend their furlough (the US Army term for leave) in separate pubs and dance halls, and fear of racial interbreeding wracked US and British authorities – but not always the British people, some of whom recognized the black soldiers as "our Allies too".

ABOVE *Until the fight across France put them in the front line, most black GIs who came to Britain worked at manual tasks such as bricklaying.*

BELOW *American GIs dancing at Rainbow Corner, the US Red Cross Club in Piccadilly which acted like a magnet to GIs when they were on "furlough" (leave) and was the envy of most British troops.*

PRISONERS OF WAR IN BRITAIN

In December 1940, Allied forces captured almost 40,000 Italians at Sidi el Barrani, near the Egyptian border with Libya. A message from the Coldstream Guards reported that they had not yet had time to count but held prisoner "about five acres of officers and two hundred acres of other ranks". By the beginning of February 1941 some 130,000 soldiers had been captured in North Africa, including several thousand colonial troops.

What was to be done with these POWs? Although the majority of Italian POWs were sent to POW camps outside the UK and most German POWs were shipped to Canada following the invasion scare of 1940–41, some POWs were used to make up the shortfall in agricultural labour that was threatening Britain's food production. The Ministry of Agriculture applied for "2,000–3,000 suitable North Italian prisoners to be brought immediately to this country in order that they may be used for urgent land reclamation work" so that the necessary crops could be grown. It seemed ironic that less than a year earlier, Italian civilians were being "collared" as inimical to the security of Britain at war, interned or deported, and now thousands of Italians who had been fighting against British troops were being shipped to the UK. Churchill had been dubious, given that there was still domestic unemployment, but by May 1941 he had conceded that it might be better to employ "docile Italians" rather than bringing over "disaffected Irish, over whom we have nothing like the same control".

Some 2,000 Italian POWs selected as suitable by the military authorities in the Middle East disembarked at Liverpool in July 1941. Most were under 30 and many had come from rural areas; though they found the British winters a great deal colder than they had been used to, the work was similar, and the farmers for whom they worked generally found their captive workforce very satisfactory.

Although at first the prisoners lived in Nissen huts and were taken in gangs to work on nearby farms, their co-operative behaviour meant that rules were soon relaxed. In January 1942 the Ministry of Agriculture announced that as an experiment, a number of "good conduct" Italian POWs would "live in" on the farm where they were working. It was an odd situation: "fraternization" (which

POWs IN THE ORKNEYS

In 1941 some 3,000 Italian POWs were sent to the Orkney Islands to build concrete barriers to protect the important Royal Navy base of Scapa Flow, despite claims that this was "work of a warlike nature" and therefore in contravention of the Geneva Convention. The War Office insisted that these concrete erections were not barriers (which they were), but rather a linking roadway for the convenience of the people of the Orkneys. For the next few years, Italians, mostly from the south, laboured on the bleak and windswept islands, eventually building a Catholic church and becoming accepted by the local people.

ABOVE In response to a request by Italian POWs working on Orkney, two Nissen huts were joined together and one of their number, Domenico Chiocchetti, gathered a team to transform them into a finely decorated Roman Catholic chapel.

LEFT Italian POWs help with the harvest on a farm "somewhere in England" on 27 August 1941. The prisoners have distinctive circles on the backs of their uniform to aid identification.

reluctant to relinquish the Italians' POW status while at the same time ignoring the restraints the Geneva Convention imposed on the type of work that POWs could do. A complicated and not very satisfactory scheme was finally worked out. Under this scheme Italians could serve in units under Italian officers which were supervised by the British. Eventually these POWs could receive more privileges over pay, letters home, leisure activities and contact with British people.

By the end of 1944 there were over 155,000 Italian POWs in the UK and thousands of Germans, captured in France, had started to arrive and needed accommodation and jobs, too. At the end of the war more than 400,000 Germans were being held in POW camps on the outskirts of most towns. By 1946 around a fifth of all farm work was being done by German POWs who were also employed on road works and housing construction, helping to rebuild the country they had been at war with for nearly six years.

" PRISONERS, therefore, while being TREATED NOT INHUMANELY, are to be shown very clearly that we regard them, Officers and men, as OUTCASTS TO THE SOCIETY OF DECENT MEN."

ADMIRALTY MEMORANDUM, JUNE 1944

in effect meant consorting with British women) had been expressly forbidden by an order published in June 1940, but this was hard to enforce when prisoners were living with a farmer's family and moving round the local area unsupervised.

The terms of the 1929 Geneva Convention (to which Britain was a signatory) specified that POWs who were officers could not be made to work, non-commissioned officers (NCOs) could only be required to work in a supervisory capacity and a private could be put to work in any capacity providing that the work was not of military importance. But of course all work contributed in some way to Britain's war effort. Wearing a distinctive circle in red, orange or yellow on the back of their uniforms to identify them, the POWs worked in forestry, limestone quarrying, iron ore mining, brickmaking, handling freight at railway stations and helping to clear bomb sites.

Their position became even more ambiguous after Italy unconditionally surrendered on 8 September 1943. By that time there were 74,900 Italian POWs in Britain and a further 11,000 were due to arrive from Algiers before the end of the year. The British government seemed to want it both ways: they were

ABOVE *German prisoners of war repair a barbed wire fence at Glen Mill POW camp, Oldham, Lancashire on Christmas Eve 1940.*

ABOVE *A regimented life. Italian POWs stand aimlessly by neatly-folded blankets on their bunks in a large, warehouse-like dormitory near London.*

RIGHT *Prisoners of War: German airmen who parachuted from a shot-down Heinkel HE 111 bomber are marched to captivity in September 1940.*

D-DAY

The long campaign for a "Second Front Now" to take the pressure off the beleaguered Russian Eastern Front was finally agreed at the Casablanca conference in January 1943. Operation OVERLORD, a large-scale landing in France, would take place the following year.

It was an operation of mind-blowing size and complexity. Plans had to be drawn up to move "something comparable to a city the size of Birmingham" across the Channel – and to keep it moving once it got to the other side. An American, General Dwight D. Eisenhower, was appointed Supreme Commander of the D-Day operations, while General Sir Bernard Montgomery was to command the land forces.

Not only was Operation OVERLORD of almost unimaginable proportions but preparations also had to be made at top speed and in the utmost secrecy. The Pas de Calais was the obvious place for a landing since it was the shortest distance from the British coast. But since it was the obvious place, the Germans had made it virtually impregnable with fortifications and gun emplacements. So the team of the Chief of Staff to the Supreme Allied Commander (COSSAC) planning D-Day settled on a stretch of the Normandy beaches further west round Caen at the foot of the Cotentin peninsula, which was much less heavily fortified.

Although details about D-Day were top secret, everyone in Britain knew that there would be an invasion of continental Europe soon and most people, for whom such an invasion could not come soon enough, were ready to help in any small way that they could. When the BBC broadcast an appeal at the request of the War Office in the winter of 1943–44 for family snapshots of the French coast to try to build up as detailed a picture of the terrain the invasion force would be facing as possible, they were overwhelmed by the response.

ABOVE A gun crew manning a Bofors gun stand ready to fire on enemy aircraft should any appear, as amphibious landing tanks are loaded on to landing craft in preparation for the cross-Channel assault on D-Day.

In conjunction with Operation OVERLORD, another operation, code-named FORTITUDE, was mounted. This was a deception plan that would feed the Germans a tissue of lies about the forthcoming invasion. Elaborate plans were laid for the Germans to "discover" a concentration of forces massing in Kent ready to launch an assault from Dover and Folkestone to Calais, whereas the troops would in fact leave from coastal resorts from Sussex through Hampshire to Dorset. Factories that had been

BELOW Building one of the Mulberry Harbours in London's East India Docks in March 1944. The floating concrete structures were towed across the Channel to provide artificial harbours on D-Day.

ABOVE *The main airborne drop in the early hours of D-Day which was intended to destroy bridges to prevent a German counter-attack was preceded by Pathfinders who would set up beacons to mark dropping zones. Here Pathfinders are synchronizing their watches before boarding their aircraft.*

manufacturing barrage balloons now turned to producing huge inflatable "tanks" which soon lined up in the fields of south-east England, while the airfields of Kent and Essex filled with plywood "planes". Dummy landing craft fashioned out of oil drums and lengths of scaffolding appeared in the Thames and Medway estuaries, and were moved around to suggest military manoeuvres. A giant rubber "oil storage tank" was constructed at Shepperton film studios and erected at Dover. To add authenticity to the deception, the King and Queen "inspected" it, as did General Eisenhower. There was also an increase in "false" radio traffic.

Meanwhile British, US and Canadian troops were in training in terrain in Cornwall, Devon, Wales and Scotland similar to that on the Normandy beaches, in the boats and DUKWs

Marching to war: British troops on the move prior to D-Day. The British people were living in a state of heightened tension throughout late May and early June knowing that the assault on "Fortress Europe", on which so much depended, could not be long in coming.

(amphibious tanks) that would take them across the Channel and on to the French beaches. The villages and hamlets in the hinterland of the beaches were cleared, and an entire village in south Devon was requisitioned for the training of US forces; in Tyneham in Dorset, villagers were evacuated at Christmas 1943 – and never allowed back.

By early May 1944 there were 2,876,600 Allied servicemen and women waiting in Britain for the liberation of north-west Europe. In the first 24 hours, 150,000 men, 1,500 tanks and 10,000 other vehicles were to be landed in Normandy, along with the supplies needed to support them, such as 1,000 gallons of drinking water.

By the end of the month, in glorious weather, the fields of southern England were crowded with the equipment of invasion. The troops, excluded from areas of military build-up, waited tensely, aware that a momentous event was about to happen.

D-Day had been fixed for 5 June 1944, but sudden appalling weather made Eisenhower delay a day. If the invasion force did not leave on 6 June, D-Day would have to be postponed for at least a fortnight, and the secrecy surrounding the operation would surely never be sustained. If the invasion failed because of adverse weather conditions in the Channel, the consequences would be too terrible to contemplate, and Eisenhower gave the order for 6 June 1944: "OK – we'll go."

FIELD MARSHAL SIR BERNARD MONTGOMERY (1887–1976)

"The whole art of war is to gain your objective with as little loss as possible," wrote Montgomery after witnessing the terrible losses of the First World War. His reputation was made in 1942 at the Battle of El Alamein in the Western Desert – the first major British land victory of the war against the Germans – and he was an outstanding, if infuriating, commander of the Allied land troops during the D-Day landings. Egotistical and arrogant, he was also a meticulous planner and an inspiration to ordinary soldiers: *"We'll hit 'em for six,"* he would say, urging his men on.

ABOVE *General Dwight D. Eisenhower, Supreme Commander, Allied Expeditionary Force on the left next to General (later Field Marshal) Sir Bernard Montgomery, meeting in London on 1 February 1944 to plan the details of the Normandy landings.*

THE V-1 AND V-2 "SECRET WEAPONS"

Exactly a week after the successful D-Day landings in Normandy, the war came to the Home Front again. In the early morning of Tuesday, 13 June 1944, a railway bridge in Bow in East London was hit, railway lines were torn up, houses and a pub were severely damaged and six people were killed, including an eight-month-old baby. The first of Hitler's "secret weapons", the V-1, an abbreviation of *Vergeltungswaffe Eins* (Retaliation Weapon One), developed as a means of extracting retribution for the Allied bombing raids on German cities, had reached its target, London.

Between then and the end of the month 2,452 V-1s, which looked like small fighter planes, were launched from fixed sites within Germany or from the air: only about 800 reached the London area; the others either crashed or were shot down by fighter planes or anti-aircraft fire. But the havoc these weapons caused was horrific. At least 499 people were known to have been killed in the first three days of the attacks and 2,000 were seriously injured. The damage to property was widespread, with 137,000 buildings being affected, because the blast power of the V-1s was far greater than that of conventional bombs. Had that rate of attacks continued, it was estimated that London would have suffered in eight weeks as great a devastation as it had endured in the nine months of the Blitz.

At first, no one knew what had hit London, although scientists had warned for some time that a deadly weapon was being developed by the Germans. Onlookers assumed that the bombs were planes that had crashed, and there were even reports of pilots baling out and being burnt to death as they catapulted to earth. It was not until three days after the first attack that it was announced on the BBC that "the enemy has started using pilotless planes against this country".

These were eerie days and deeply distressing to the morale of people, who had believed that the war must be nearly over now that the Allies had begun the fight back across occupied Europe. Between 100 and 150 V-1s were aimed at London every day along a pre-set path and the alerts came so frequently that confusion fused with fear. There would be an intense whining, humming sound, followed, when the engine cut out, by a terrifying silence before the bomb plunged to the ground and exploded. The Home Secretary, Herbert Morrison, suggested that rather than calling the

ABOVE *The devastation caused by a V-2 rocket bomb in Limehouse in east London in March 1945. In the foreground a man examines the propulsion unit.*

V-1s "pilotless planes", which made them seem particularly sinister, the V-1s should be referred to as "flying bombs", but "doodlebugs" was what most people called them. Many dispirited Londoners left the city; by 1 September over a million in the "priority class" (school-aged children, mothers with infants under five, expectant mothers, the aged and infirm) had been evacuated. Many more took advantage of a scheme by which evacuees were entitled to free travel warrants and billeting allowances.

The worst single incident of the V-1 campaign occurred on 18 June, when a V-1 landed on the Guards' Chapel at Wellington Barracks while a service was in progress, killing 121 people including 63 soldiers. On 30 June, a V-1 landed on the Aldwych in central London and killed 48; 45 people were killed in Kensington on 28 July and on that same "Black Friday" 51 were killed and 151 seriously injured when a V-1 fell on Lewisham in south London.

BELOW *The crew of a twin-Browning light anti-aircraft gun keep watch for V-1 flying bombs on 19 June 1944.*

By 7 September 1944, the V-1 attacks had petered out to such an extent that the government announced that the "battle for London" was virtually over. However, the V-1 attacks had decreased because Germany had a more effective weapon, whose technical difficulties had now been resolved and which forced labour had produced. The next day, the second of Hitler's "secret weapons" arrived. The V-2 was a massive 14-metre- (46-foot)-long rocket packed with a ton of explosives, launched from still-occupied Holland and Walcheren. There was no siren alert, no time to take cover, but it was not until 11 November 1944 that the press was permitted to tell the British population what they already knew. It was not "gas main explosions" but "the most indiscriminate weapon of this or any other war" that was bringing unprecedented damage to property as well as death, injury and terror to a population that had already endured five years of war. Between 8 September 1944 and 27 March 1945, when the last V-2 fell in Kent, a total of 1,054 V-2 rockets fell on England – an average of five a day – but only a total of 517, or less than three a day, reached their intended target, London. These "reprisal weapons" brought the Germans no strategic advantage despite the devastation they caused, and attacks petered out as British counter-measures grew more effective and the Germans withdrew their launching troops in the face of the Allied advance.

LEFT *A V-2, a gyroscopically-stabilized finned rocket, 14 metres (46 feet) long, weighed just under four tons without fuel. The direction was preset, its maximum range was between 320 and 350 kilometres (200–220 miles), and it reached a maximum speed of 5,800 kilometres (3,600 miles) an hour.*

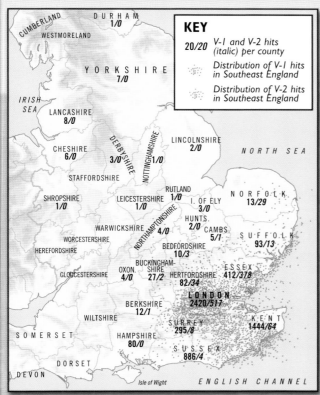

KEY

20/20   V-1 and V-2 hits (italic) per county

Distribution of V-1 hits in Southeast England

Distribution of V-2 hits in Southeast England

CUMBERLAND 1/0
DURHAM 1/0
WESTMORELAND
YORKSHIRE 7/0
IRISH SEA
LANCASHIRE 8/0
CHESHIRE 6/0
DERBYSHIRE 3/0
NOTTINGHAMSHIRE 1/0
LINCOLNSHIRE 2/0
NORTH SEA
STAFFORDSHIRE
SHROPSHIRE 1/0
LEICESTERSHIRE 1/0
RUTLAND 1/0
I. OF ELY 3/0
NORFOLK 13/29
WARWICKSHIRE 4/0
NORTHAMPTONSHIRE 4/0
HUNTS. 2/0
CAMBS. 5/1
SUFFOLK 93/13
WORCESTERSHIRE
HEREFORDSHIRE
BEDFORDSHIRE 10/3
BUCKINGHAMSHIRE 27/2
OXON. 4/0
HERTFORDSHIRE 82/34
ESSEX 412/378
GLOUCESTERSHIRE
LONDON 2420/517
BERKSHIRE 12/1
KENT 1444/64
WILTSHIRE
SURREY 295/8
SOMERSET
HAMPSHIRE 80/0
SUSSEX 886/4
DORSET
DEVON
Isle of Wight
ENGLISH CHANNEL

"V" WEAPON ATTACKS ON BRITAIN

- *Over 10,000 V-1 flying bombs were launched against England; 7,488 of them crossed the British coast, of which 3,957 were shot down before reaching their target. Of the 3,351 remaining, 2,420 reached London and around 30 fell on Southampton and Portsmouth. The furthest reach of a V-1 was Manchester and Oldham (these were air launched). V-1s killed 6,184 people and injured 17,981.*
- *A total of 1,054 V-2 rockets fell on England, 517 of these reaching London, where they killed a total of 2,754 people and injured 6,523.*
- *In total 23,000 homes were destroyed by V-1 and V-2 bombs.*

RIGHT *A Civil Defence warden comforts a terrified child who has just been rescued by a fireman from a house hit by a V-1 flying bomb in southern England on 23 June 1944.*

THE END: VE DAY AND VJ DAY

Peace came slowly. The fight back across western Europe was beset with reverses and in December 1944 the German Army mounted a surprise offensive in the Ardennes. It lasted a month and was unsuccessful, but claimed some 80,000 Allied casualties. By the beginning of February 1945, the Russian army was within 40 miles of Berlin and at the Yalta Conference that month, America, Britain and Russia struggled to work out the details of a post-war settlement. Roosevelt died on 12 April 1945 and the Allies liberated the concentration camps of Auschwitz, Buchenwald and Belsen on 27 January, 11 and 15 April 1945 respectively. Stark newsreels of the unimaginable atrocities perpetrated at these camps were shown to stunned audiences in British and American cinemas.

On 30 April 1945, Hitler committed suicide in the ruins of his bunker in Berlin and on 4 May the German forces in north-west Europe surrendered to Montgomery at his HQ on Lüneberg Heath. On 7 May the German Supreme Command surrendered at the Supreme Headquaters Allied Expeditionary Forces (SHAEF) in Rheims in northern France. The war in Europe was over.

After some debate among the Allies, it was announced that the following day, 8 May 1945, would be celebrated as VE (Victory in Europe) Day in Britain. Flags had already begun to appear in windows, bunting was being draped across the streets, and souvenir sellers were out in force.

Although there were no official plans for the celebrations, London acted as a magnet for a war-weary people who were determined to allow themselves "a brief period of rejoicing", as Churchill would advise later that day, before facing up to the realities of the peace. Thousands, many wearing their best clothes, surged along the streets wondering where to go and what to do, stopping to have a drink in a pub, breaking into song, linking arms

ABOVE *St Paul's Cathedral, symbol of the indomitable spirit of the Blitz, is caught in a "V for Victory" by searchlights beaming on the dome on VE Day.*

THE ATOMIC BOMB

On 6 August 1945, the first operational atomic bomb was dropped on the Japanese city of Hiroshima, reducing an area of 13 square kilometres (5 square miles) to ashes. Probably around 140,000 people were killed, either then or in the months and years after, and there were catastrophic effects on those who survived and on their unborn children. Three days later a second A-bomb was dropped on the city of Nagasaki, this time killing around 73,884, injuring 74,909, and causing the same long-term radiation effects. Japan surrendered on 14 August and the new terror weapon rewrote the working of the post-war balance of power.

RIGHT *The devastation caused by one of the atomic bombs dropped on Japan in 1945. It is unclear whether this is Hiroshima or Nagasaki since the scene is one of almost total destruction (although the expanse of flat land suggests Hiroshima).*

for a dance. At 15:00 all fell silent as Churchill's broadcast from Downing Street was relayed to the crowds through loudspeakers – as it was throughout much of the country. The Prime Minister gave a brief reprise of the war, starting with the "whole year" when Britain and the Empire had "maintained the struggle single-handed". He paid tribute to the military might of the Soviet Union and to the "overwhelming power and resources of the United States of America" before bringing his brief history to an end: "finally almost the whole world was combined against the evil-doers who are now prostrate before us… Advance Britannia! Long live the cause of freedom! God save the King!" he urged and his voice faltered.

Churchill's car, with the great man standing in the back giving his "V for Victory" sign, was mobbed on its way to the Commons where Churchill thanked MPs for "their noble support during the war years" and led them in a short service of remembrance at St Margaret's for the 21 MPs killed during the war.

Soon after 17:00 the Prime Minister spoke to the crowds directly from the balcony of the Ministry of Health. "This is your hour," he told them. "This is your victory." "For He's a Jolly Good Fellow," the crowd roared back. Later, Churchill appeared on the balcony of Buckingham Palace with the King and Queen, who made a series of appearances that night, sometimes with their daughters, the Princesses Elizabeth and Margaret Rose.

While the blackout did not officially end until two days later – on 10 May – all over Britain bonfires lit up the night sky, many burning effigies of Hitler, and people ate and drank, danced and sang. Those who could tried to forget how it had been for nearly six years. Those who could not mourned family and friends dead, wounded, missing or in POW camps.

The next day was a public holiday, too, with lots of street parties for the children using rations that had been carefully hoarded for just this moment. Then it was back to everyday life, and wondering how much longer the fighting would go on in the Far East and thinking how distressing the news was filtering back of how the prisoners of the Japanese were suffering.

When Japan surrendered on 14 August 1945, Winston Churchill had been replaced in a General Election by Clement Attlee. "The last of our enemies is laid low," Attlee wrote, and again there was a two-day public holiday on 15–16 August to celebrate VJ (Victory over Japan) Day. George VI rode with his Queen in a golden coach to the State Opening of Parliament and from the throne announced that the coal mines and the Bank of England would be nationalized by his new Labour government.

A NEW JERUSALEM?

On VE Day, Churchill had followed his injunction to rejoice with a warning: "Let us not forget for a moment the toil and effort that lie ahead". At the end of the Second World War, Britain had emerged from the struggle victorious but deeply in debt, battered, shabby, exhausted and with few resources left. US Lend Lease was withdrawn a week after Japan surrendered on 21 August 1945, by which time Britain had "borrowed" over £5 billion-worth of goods from the US. The economist John Maynard Keynes was dispatched to Washington and an agreement was hammered out setting repayment at £162 million. This meant that in the early post-war years almost everything that Britain produced would have to go for export.

In November 1946, an exhibition was held at the Victoria and Albert Museum in London, whose own exhibits were still in wartime storage, to show that British manufacturers were capable of producing "goods as suitable for peacetime as were the weapons the country produced for war". The exhibition was an outstanding success, drawing crowds from all over the country. But all too soon "Britain Can Make It", as the exhibition had been called, was being modified to "But Britain Can't Have It".

If manufactured goods were unavailable to the domestic market, so was almost everything else. Bread, which had never been rationed during the war, was rationed in July 1946. By 1948, rations had fallen well below wartime averages and that winter even potatoes were rationed; meat was down to 1s 0d (5p) worth per person per week, along with 45g (1½oz) of cheese, 1.2 litres (two pints) of milk and a single egg. And there were other restricted foods. Indeed, things were so dire that when the much-disliked wartime staple dried egg powder was withdrawn from the shops, there was an immediate campaign for its return. Clothes were rationed until May 1949; the French couturier Christian Dior's 1947 "New Look", with its long, full skirts, was something that most British women, in their skimpy, functional "utility clothes", could only dream about. It was not until 1954 that rationing was abolished.

There was an acute post-war fuel crisis and in the bitter winter of 1946–47 the hours when you could turn on an electric fire were strictly controlled. Domestic coal had to be eked out with great ingenuity, and shortages and transport difficulties had thrown 1.75 million men out of work by February 1947.

BELOW *Welcome Home. An enthusiastic reception for Sergeant F. Tucker from his wife, young son and flag-waving villagers when he returned from a German POW camp to Oreston, south Devon, a week after VE Day.*

RIGHT *"A war worth winning". Abram Games's poster of a new Britain rising from the ruins of war.*

BELOW *Building a new Britain. Two soldiers brush up on their brick-laying skills in Cairo while on a vocational course offered to men awaiting demobilization and a return to their pre-war trades in "civvy street".*

It was clear that many who had served in Armed Forces would return to find their homes had been destroyed or rendered uninhabitable by enemy action and the housing shortage would be acute: 3.25 million properties had been destroyed, 92 per cent of which were private dwellings, and half of which were in London. Thousands more were in a poor state of repair. The Minister of Health and Housing, Aneurin Bevan, had promised to build "five million homes in quick time", a rash promise he was unable to fulfil, given the shortage of materials and labour. The crisis was eased somewhat by 150,000 "prefab" (pre-fabricated) houses. These proved to be far from the short-term solution that had been intended, with some lasting until the end of the twentieth century.

The basis of demobilization was largely length of service, and men had been promised that their jobs would be waiting for them when they came home to "civvy street". But this was not always possible: firms took time to get back to peacetime production, some had closed down and materials were short. It also meant that many women who had been drawn into the labour market in wartime would have to move out to accommodate the returning men. Some were happy to return to domestic life after the strains of war, but many would have liked to work part-time, and others wanted to hold on to their wartime jobs but were denied the opportunity to do so.

"Austerity" was the only possible description for post-war Britain. But within those bleak years lay a blueprint for a new Jerusalem of greater equality and opportunity than had been most people's lot in pre-war decades. This new Jerusalem had many parts: there was the National Health Service Act, passed in 1946, and the NHS itself, launched 5 July 1948 and initially free to all at the point of delivery, along with a house-building programme that, if slow to get going, had delivered by 1953, and spawned a number of "new towns" away from city slums. There was also the nationalization of some of Britain's key industries, including coal mining and the railways; and the concept of "parity of esteem" enshrined in the 1944 Education Act. Above all, the new Jerusalem recognized that wartime sacrifice earned peacetime entitlements – for everyone.

> **" The GREAT SOCIETY has arrived and the task of OUR GENERATION is to bring it UNDER CONTROL."**
>
> **ANEURIN BEVAN, POST-WAR LABOUR MINISTER OF HEALTH AND HOUSING.**

COMING HOME

Although demobilization was based on length of service, those who had skills urgently needed for post-war reconstruction, such as house building, were fast-tracked home to Britain, to collect their "demob" suit and resume life in "civvy street". It was not always an easy transition: more than two million women had been without their husbands for the duration of the war, and children had grown up without fathers. Family life had to be relearned and wartime transgressions overlooked: the divorce rate, which had been 10,000 a year in 1938, shot up to 25,000 in 1945, of which 70 per cent were sought on the grounds of adultery.

ABOVE *An airgraph showing a girl's enthusiasm for the demobilization of her father used to illustrate an article by Pearl Binder about "Re-introducing Father to the family and vice versa" in* Housewife, *November 1944.*

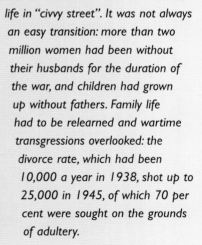

61

INDEX

Figures in *italics* denote illustrations